THE CRAFT OF THE
letter

By Michael Casson
Edited by Anna Jackson

1 Tzu Chou Sung stoneware bottle with brush-painted decoration
on white slip, 10th-12th century China.

BRITISH BROADCASTING CORPORATION

Editor's note

This book has been written as a result of the response we received to the BBC television series *'The Craft of the Potter'*, first transmitted in April 1976. In the programmes we tried to help the viewer not only to make a pot, but to make a better pot, by referring to the finest examples of historical and contemporary work; some of our most notable modern potters, such as David Leach, Alan Caiger-Smith, Mary Rogers and Walter Keeler contributed by showing their techniques and by giving an insight into the aesthetics behind these techniques. These contributions have found their way into this book and Lynne Reeve, who appeared in the programme, has written the section on glazes from her extensive knowledge and research. We are grateful for the help of the Crafts Advisory Committee in the preparation of the text.

Making this series was a very happy experience for me: I was greatly helped by those with whom I worked; I discovered that potters are an unusual and varied group of people, for many of whom pottery-making is not merely a means of earning a living, but is inseparable from a craftsman's way of life where work, art and leisure come together. Above all it was a great pleasure to work on the series, and now on this book, with Michael Casson, a talented potter from whom I learned much.

Anna Jackson

Published to accompany a series of programmes prepared in consultation with the BBC Further Education Advisory Council

Published by the British Broadcasting Corporation 35 Marylebone High Street London W 1M 4AA

ISBN 0 563 16127 2

First published 1977
© The Author 1977

Printed in England by Garnett Print, Rotherham and London

This book is set in 12 on 13pt Times Roman Photon

2 Pedestal bowl, unglazed earthenware with painted decoration, 800 BC Cyprus.

Contents

Numbers in the text refer to illustrations. Roman numbers correspond to action
pictures; italic numbers indicate an historical or contemporary pot.

Preface

The world seems made for potters. Earth, water and fire are the basic elements of this craft that has been part of man's life since earliest times. In recent years more and more people both as amateurs and professionals have been rediscovering the pleasures of working with clay; it gives the satisfaction of creating a unique piece of work in an age of mass production. Pottery has form, colour, texture, and often has a direct function so that we may cook in it, eat and drink from it. It demands a response from our senses as well as our minds; you can touch it, pick it up and feel it in your hands. I have seen many people who have come to understand more about themselves through making things with clay and fire.

The range of possibilities is very wide; this book is about the dozens of processes that potters, past and present, go through to make functional pots, decorative objects and ceramic sculpture. It tells you how to begin but it also has plenty for the more expert. It leads from making – handbuilding and throwing – to finishing, that is decorating and glazing and firing. The last chapter has an outline guide to the achievements of potters from the earliest times to the present day. This historical survey should be read with the rest of the book in mind because the examples mentioned are specifically chosen to illustrate technical and aesthetic points referred to in previous chapters. Moreover the photographs of historical and contemporary work are selected to show both technical processes and aesthetic solutions to particular ways of working.

You may come across unfamiliar technical terms – when potters get together they often seem to have a language of their own – the glossary on page 126 will explain them. Further reading has been suggested in the Booklist. I should like to stress the importance of both taking notes and recording experiments. Pottery takes time, clay dries slowly, kilns fire over many hours and it is asking too much just to remember all the things you learn as you go along. Keep accurate accounts of all you do: how you make up the materials you use, how you use them, their measurements and relative strengths. Time spent in this way is repaid by a growing sense of understanding of the materials and processes of this fascinating craft.

Many potters, young and old, have helped me to make better pots in the past 30 years; I hope that this book will be useful to beginners, and perhaps also stimulate those more experienced.

Michael Casson

The Author

Michael Casson has been making pots for about 30 years. For much of this time he has combined the production of wheel-made functional work with teaching – all ages from 7 to 70+! During the last few years, however, he has been concentrating exclusively on making more individual pieces in high-fired stoneware and porcelain.

For him the main fascination and fulfilment of pottery comes from a response to the wide variety of materials – clays, rocks etc – available to the potter, as well as the process of throwing, decorating and firing pots. Over the years he has played an active part in the various Craft Societies set up to help craftsmen. He was a founder member of the Craftsmen Potters Association and co-founder with Victor Margrie of Harrow Studio Pottery course; he is an Adviser to the Crafts Advisory Committee and sits on the Board of Dartington Pottery Workshop Training Scheme. He has had work exhibited widely in Great Britain and other parts of the world; most private and public collections have examples of his work.

Photography by Ed Buziak

Drawings by Ray and Corrine Burrows

Acknowledgement is due to the following for permission to reproduce photographs:–

ASHMOLEAN MUSEUM, OXFORD plate 349; BRITISH MUSEUM plate 285; JANE COPER plate 293; CRAFTS ADVISORY COMMITTEE colour plate 5 and back cover plate 2; DAVID CRIPPS plate 405 and colour plate 15; PETER DICK plates 51 and 52; MICHAEL HOLFORD plates 100 and 408; JAPAN FOLK ART MUSEUM plate 302; ERIC MELLON colour plate 8; PAUL NORBURY PUBLICATIONS LTD. plate 125; ORIENTAL INSTITUTE, UNIVERSITY OF CHICAGO plate 124; JACQUELINE PONCELET plate 288; SMITHSONIAN INSTITUTION, FREER GALLERY OF ART, WASHINGTON D.C. plate 318; STOKE-ON-TRENT CITY MUSEUMS plate 431; VICTORIA AND ALBERT MUSEUM plates 1, 58, 104, 118, 191, 289, 291, 301, 308, 312, 345, 347, 348, 364, 368, 400, 403, 406, 409, 410, 411, 412, 413, 415, 417, 419, 429, colour plates 10 and 13; BARRY VINCENT plate 404; THE TRUSTEES OF THE WALLACE COLLECTION colour plate 4; JOSIAH WEDGWOOD & SONS LTD. plate 314; YAMATO BUNKAKAN MUSEUM, NARA plate 416.

Acknowledgement is due to the following for permission to include pots, photographed by Ed Buziak:–

BLACKMAN HARVEY LTD. plate 427; BRITISH MUSEUM (MUSEUM OF MANKIND) plates 109, 110, 365, 422, 423, 424, 425 and 428; CASSON GALLERY plates 57, 75, 99, 103, 283, 290, 307, 343, 369, 371 and 399; MICHAEL AND SHEILA CASSON plates 123, 271, 310, 313, 346, 356, 396, 402 and colour plate 18; JON AND KATE CATLEUGH plate 292; CRAFTS ADVISORY COMMITTEE plates 114, 122, 309, 370, 372, 373, 430, colour plates 12 and 17; PAN CASSON HENRY plates 3, 298, 328, 367, 426 and colour plate 7; HORNIMAN MUSEUM plates 17, 420 and back cover plate 4; ANNA JACKSON plates 91, 421 and back cover plate 1; DAPHNE SWAN plate 270; VICTORIA AND ALBERT MUSEUM plates 2, 115, 303, 336, 407, 418, colour plates 1, 2, 3, 6, 9, 14, 16, 20 and back cover plate 5.

The remaining photographs were specially taken for the BBC by ED BUZIAK.

What is clay?

Clay is a joy to handle. Sometimes it is gritty and earthy inviting a vigorous, robust response, but it can also have a smooth, silky quality that lends itself to a delicate touch. It has many colours, that come from the minerals in the clays themselves or from the slips and glazes that coat the pots and make them rough or smooth, matt or shiny. Clay is all around us, it is relatively cheap and you can make just about any kind of form with it – from bricks to teacups, clay pipes to clay models. It can be used as a liquid, as a soft, malleable material, or you can join it together in a leather-hard state. Painter, sculptor, craftsman, artist – a potter can be a little of all these – geologist, chemist, engineer, even businessman as well, and will approach his clay accordingly. Some potters I know delve deeply into the chemical and physical structure of their clay, while others simply take it straight out of the bag and use it without a thought for its composition or origin. I personally believe that certain very basic facts can be both interesting and helpful, whatever your particular bias may be.

Origins of clay

The raw materials of pottery are found abundantly all over the world because the granite-type igneous rocks from which they ultimately derive account for most of the earth's crust. The hard igneous rocks are decomposed by hot gases from the bowels of the earth into a soft rock containing the feldspar minerals. Millions of years' exposure to weathering by rain, sun and ice break down some of these feldspars into the 'primary clays' which are always found where they are formed. The China clays of St Austell in Cornwall are a good example; they are white, free from impurities, large in particle size and therefore relatively 'non-plastic'. When these primary or 'mother' clays are transported by the natural forces of wind, glaciers, rivers or seas they pick up impurities like iron and other minerals, as well as much organic matter. Their journey pounds, crushes and further weathers them, until by the time they are finally laid down, often thousands of miles from their place of origin, they are changed in colour, texture and particle size. They have become what we call 'plastic'.

3 Tall bottle, stoneware with sgraffito decoration through an iron-bearing slip by David Leach.

Plasticity is something to do with the flat hexagonal shape of the clay particles and their size – it's still something of a mystery, but they hold water between them, and, like sheets of wet glass they allow movement, and so shape, by slipping and sliding without coming apart. The smaller the particle the more plastic the clay. As the water dries out they stop sliding and go rigid. So clay retains its shape, even when it is fired to a good red heat as it undergoes a chemical and physical change to become a relatively hard and durable material.

When the water dries out it will cause the clay to shrink, the usual rate is 12% or 1 in 8, but some clays shrink excessively, even to 17% or more, which can cause warping or even cracking. The potter must accept the fact that his pot will get smaller from the moment it is made to when finally it is fired in the kiln; he must overcome the clay's tendency to warp by the proper use of the right materials.

Types of Clay

The two *primary* or *residual* clays that most concern the potter are *China clays* and *bentonite* – a sticky, very finely particled and therefore highly plastic clay (capable of giving plasticity to a non-plastic clay by the addition of only 3% to 5%).

All the others are designated *secondary* or *sedimentary* clays, and they include the low-firing red clays suitable for earthenware, as well as the fireclays and stoneware clays that withstand much higher temperatures. In fact the ability to fire to certain temperatures without distorting is another way of classifying clays:

Refractory clays: the primary China clays and some of the fireclays from which high-temperature kiln bricks are made. Either of these clays can be added if temperatures of say 1250°C or upwards are needed.

Vitrifiable clays: clays which can fire to the point where the particles are fused together without distortion of the form. Good stoneware clays will do this, and of course, porcelain is vitrified.

4 Tear the piece in half with a twisting action.

Fusible clays: these are the lower-firing clays which are used mainly for earthenwares because they would actually melt before they reached 1300°C.

So it is clear that there are many different types of clays with greatly varying properties. It is rare that a potter can go and dig a clay out of the ground and use it just like that for the work that is to be made; these clays, together with other minerals such as sand, feldspars, quartz and perhaps grog (fired and ground clay), must be blended to form the 'body' suitable for all the potter's requirements of colour, texture and temperature.

The three main types of pottery are:

Earthenware, fired from 700°C approximately at its very lowest, up to when it starts to vitrify, at about 1200°C; to go beyond this point would usually cause deforming or would produce a pot that fractures easily. (Industry has confused the issue somewhat by producing a vitrified, light-coloured earthenware which is fired to a high temperature on the first firing (biscuit), but then to a lower firing to fix the glaze. Much industrially made earthenware is of this type).

5/6 Bring the pieces smartly together.

Traditional earthenware is porous, i.e. the particles are not fused together, and it needs glazing all over to make it non-porous. Its virtue, besides the obvious saving on fuel at these low temperatures, is that, in addition to the normal range of colours, you can get some brilliant effects derived from oxides which would not stand a higher temperature *(colour 11, colour 18, 2, 290).*

Stoneware, fired from about 1200°C to 1300°C; this is a hard, non-porous material that only needs glazing for hygienic or aesthetic reasons, since the particles are fused and vitrified. Here the total effect can be one of subdued, subtle integration of clays and glazes. Only a smaller number of oxides will stand the hot fire. Stoneware is a favourite with studio potters, who enjoy the challenge of a narrower but deeper range of possibilities *(colour 12, colour 17, 1, 3, 419).*

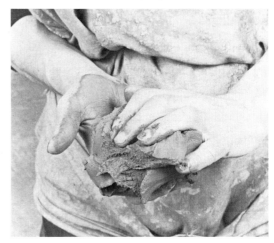

Porcelain, also extremely hard and non-porous – fired between 1250°C and very high temperatures in the 1400°C area and beyond for some industrial porcelains. Porcelain bodies contain china clay, feldspar and quartz usually with some bentonite if they are to be thrown on the wheel. It is not particularly plastic, so it is not easy to throw with, and it usually needs turning. It distorts easily and you must plan your forms to take this into account. Its main attraction besides its hard, white quality is that if thin enough it will be translucent *(back cover 3).* You don't generally go to porcelain for a robust pot, but you will get elegance, and some of the most beautiful pieces in the world *(400, 289, back cover 5).*

Stages in making a pot

Although some potters only fire once ('raw firing') the generally accepted procedure that potters follow is: *prepare* the clay body; make the *form*; thoroughly *dry* it out; *fire* it to 'biscuit'; *glaze* it and *fire* it again. *Decoration* can come in at any of these stages, even after the second firing (when another firing will be necessary to fix the decoration on the glaze, e.g. enamels).

Preparation of clay

Clay can be bought in lump form, which has to be crushed or soaked down before it can be used, or as a powder, ready to be mixed with water and other materials. More conveniently for the beginner, you can buy it in 'plastic' form, i.e. soft and damp and ready to use. This will come in a polythene bag which should be kept moist inside, sealed and then stored in a cool place. Even this ready-prepared clay body will need some attention before you use it. *Wedging* is the most commonly used method, and small lumps of clay can be torn off and banged together in the hands to exclude the air in what is called *hand wedging* (4-6). Usually, though, larger lumps of perhaps 10-40 lb (4½ to 19 kilos) are cut in half and banged down on top of each other on the bench in a continuous cut, bang, turn; cut, bang, turn rhythm (7-11). It is essential that the clay should be soft. Wedging not only excludes the air and makes the lump even in texture, it tends to dry out the clay as well: if the clay is slightly hard to start with, wedging will only make matters worse. This applies even more to *kneading*, the other main method of preparation, because one of the aims is to bring all the clay into contact with the bench, usually made of some absorbent material like wood, so that air bubbles burst as the clay is constantly turned over and compressed. Kneading is almost impossible to describe in words but it is a two handed rhythmic action that brings the inside clay in the lump being kneaded to the outside, continually turning the mass inside out as it were. David Leach who takes his clay directly from a dough-mixing machine (that mixes the

7 Bring the clay down with controlled force.

8 Lift and turn on its side.

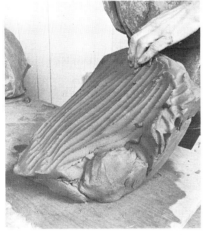

9 Draw the clay up to eliminate cracks and seams in the surface which might trap air.

10 Cut in half with a stout wire.

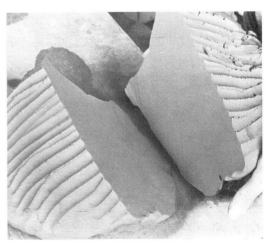

11 Result: well-mixed clay, no air-bubbles.

powdered ingredients with water) gives each lump, maybe 20-30 lb or more (9-13 kilos), one hundred kneading 'turns' before he considers it ready for use. You can use two main hand grips on the lump to be kneaded: **i)** both hands equally spaced at each end of a short thick roll of clay, push down and slightly inwards with the palms applying equal pressure; the fingers control and gather in the ends of the lump as they tend to spread outwards. This method forms the *oxface* or *ramshead* shape (12). **ii)** the *spiral,* even more difficult to describe, is where one hand is below the other; one hand is more dominant in its pushing down action than the other and the total rhythmic push-lift-and-twist action keeps the clay rotating on the same spot resulting in a spirally twisted cone of clay (13-15). Many potters believe this method places the clay particles in a spiral alignment that will help when the clay is thrown on the wheel. This can only be true of course if the whole lump is used. But kneading certainly conditions the clay, and taken slowly and rhythmically prepares the potter for the work ahead. Throwers particularly find kneading an important prelude to work on the wheel, resting and concentrating the mind.

12 Kneading: 'ox-face'.

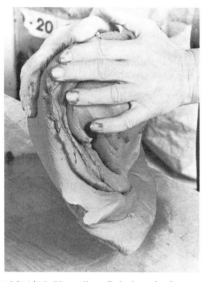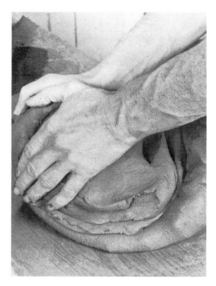

13/14/15 Kneading: Spiral method.

Generally speaking when beginning handbuilding or throwing have the clay soft – get the feel of it first so that it moves easily in your hands. Later you will learn about the different hardnesses suitable for different procedures. If the clay is too hard, knock it all into a lump and cut this into bread-and-butter slices with a wire, and making small dimples in each slice, lower them into a bowl of water and put them back together again in a lump (16). Don't be in too much of a hurry, let the water soak through for at least 10 minutes before you get your fingers into it, and first by the hand method and then by wedging knock it back into condition, free of air and much softer. If you have to add sand or grog to a clay it is best done with a little water in a similar way; the water will prevent sand or grog drying out the clay too much. If clay has gone bone hard then break it up into small pieces and simply sprinkle water onto it and let it soak through for a day or so, adding more water if necessary. If clay is too soft to work, it has either to be left out in the air, preferably in arched thick rope shapes, or if really too sloppy then run it onto some absorbent surface like plaster of Paris or thick asbestos board. (Keep a good eye on this way of drying slurry and get to it long before a hard crust forms on the side next to the drying slab. Turn it over several times before you remove it for wedging). Clay bodies for handbuilding or throwing need different properties, and are dealt with later. Finally clay does not deteriorate, it improves with age. Some potters store their clays for years, especially porcelain which needs a long time to improve its throwing properties. Wedge it into good condition, and keep it moist in its bag so that it stays that way.

16 Softening clay.

Handbuilding

People have been using clay to make models of animals and human figures for at least as long as they've been painting on cave walls. As they settled down to grow crops and raise livestock, the earliest farmer potters began to make functional vessels, for storing food and to bury the ashes of their dead (*403*). These earliest pots were all made without the use of the wheel, and these same handbuilding methods continue to be used by many potters today. Some of the most beautiful pots in the world have been handbuilt.

There are no rules for making handbuilt forms. As long as you allow the clay to be used in a sympathetic way, add and join pieces at the right time – and all that means is that they stay put and don't come apart later – then the imagination has a completely free rein to explore and invent. There are favourite tools and well-tried methods but they are not exclusive, and you may get your ideas for shape and form from anywhere. Mary Rogers (25), who makes delicate handbuilt forms, uses very few tools and her main methods are pinching, coiling and wrap-around; her inspiration comes from looking at natural objects such as flowers and fruit (18); look about you and see the sort of shapes that interest you in nature, or look at non wheel-made forms that have a specific function, such as coiled or slab-built plant pots, or lasagne dishes for the kitchen. Nature or function can be the starting point for making, and either purely sculptural forms or highly usable pots are all within the compass of handbuilding methods.

17 Modelled horseman from Cyprus, 9th century BC.

18 Mary Rogers' pots take their inspiration from natural forms, a flower, a shell, the broken line of a mountain range.

Tools for handbuilding

Some handbuilders use nothing but their hands whilst others have a bewildering array of tools, aids, supports and the like. Here are a few of the most usual tools found on the handbuilder's bench. First perhaps you have no bench, well then a *wooden board* or piece of hardboard is essential, any smooth-grained slightly absorbent surface will do. Since much flattening and pressing will go on there, you will need a *rolling pin*, and a *fine-pointed knife* (19) to cut out shapes and slabs. You will probably need a *pin mounted on a stick* (20) to trim away uneven clay. Then there are a whole host of *scraping implements* (21): surfaces in handbuilding can have great variety, and hacksaw blades, metal kidneys, serrated-edged shells, old (backed) razor blades, combs of wood or metal all help to achieve this. *Boxwood modelling tools* (22) come in all shapes and sizes – you will find them useful for smoothing and joining clay. You can impress patterns on the clay by rolling it out on *strips of cloth* or *heavier textured material*, or you can stamp or mark the clay with *found objects* of all kinds from buttons to bones. Anything goes, in the Pandora's Box of the handbuilder's equipment; for the handbuilder, even more than for the thrower, the selection of tools becomes a highly personal choice. In Japan, for example, the potters strengthen their shapes with *textured beaters* made of wood which at the same time apply a decorative surface to the work (23). Another potter from a Papuan village may use a carefully chosen smooth river stone which he repeatedly throws into a lump of soft clay to expand the form outwards larger and larger (24), whilst a British handbuilder I know uses an inflated balloon covered with an old silk stocking onto which she presses the clay form. More tools and special equipment will crop up in the rest of this chapter.

Clays for handbuilding

The more experience you have, the more you will respond to certain types of clays, until you realise that they can all be used once you accept their limitations. The catalogues of the suppliers show all kinds, from the ultra-smooth porcelains to the coarse-grained 'crank' mixtures. You can experiment in blending these while they are soft so that, for example, the colour of one clay can be added to the strength of another. Always make tests. Many catalogues will list a particular body as suitable for handbuilding, but you may want to alter its consistency. To begin with a sandy open clay body will give you fewer problems, so you may want to add between 8%-12% fine silica sand to any earthenware or stoneware body (26-30); this will be more responsive to your touch and dry out better (even though the walls of your forms may be uneven in thickness) with less warping in the kiln.

Remember that time must be made to work for you in handbuilding: no matter which clay or process you use, you can seldom finish a form straight away because the walls will get too floppy. Have several pieces on the go at once, letting each one dry a little until you can continue without loss of shape. Thin plastic bags are most useful here for either keeping work as moist as you left it or for gradually letting it dry out, depending on how thoroughly you wrap things up.

Pinching

Pinch-, or thumb-pots, as some people call them, are probably the easiest and most immediate way to start to handbuild. Mary Rogers says: 'Pinch building is a very quiet and satisfying activity. The work proceeds slowly and rhythmically, and it is all done entirely within the two hands. The best approach is one of relaxed concentration, in fact it is an advantage not to hurry, because during the pinching out the warmth of

19 Potter's knife, can also be ground down to thinner blade.

20 Pin mounted on a stick.

21 Metal scraping tool.

22 Boxwood modelling tool.

23 Textured wooden beaters.

24 Papuan potter using a river-stone to shape the inside of the pot.

25 Mary Rogers is a potter who specialises in hand-building, mainly pinching and coiling delicate forms made in translucent porcelain. Her ceramics have been exhibited widely in Britain and abroad.

the hands stiffens the clay, so that it loses its floppiness and begins to hold the shape that you give it.

'The "organic" quality of a good pinched pot is one of its attractive features; slight variations of curve and balance are a natural feature of every pinched form. These occur because of the way in which the pots are made. A pinched pot starts with a ball of clay which is only roughly spherical, and the first opening up with the thumb is only roughly central, so that, from the beginning, there are slight differences of wall thickness, which will give slight variations of wall height and curvature in the finished piece. This is the basis of the difference between a pinch-built and a wheel-thrown form, in which the clay is first centred exactly, and then caused to create its volume evenly about a central axis.

'Another characteristic of pinch-built pots, arising from the way in which they are formed, is the more or less indented surface where the fingers have left their impression. This surface texture can be left, especially where it occurs in a decorative manner, and it seems especially suitable with rough and groggy clays, but with fine pieces, such as those made in porcelain, a smooth and highly refined surface often seems to be preferable.' (Mary Rogers pots – *45, 56, 73, 91, 95, back cover 3*.)

Whether your pot is to be thick or thin, plan out the form from the base upwards. First make your ball of soft clay, patting it into shape between your hands; even the shape of this ball has a determining factor on the outcome (31). Before you plunge in your thumb you must *decide* what kind of form you are aiming at. That is the moment of decision. Wider shapes have flatter, wider bases. Pinch and stroke between the fingers and thumb in a rhythmic way, going round and round the pot.

Some potters find it helpful to keep moistening their fingers, especially when using coarser clays, and the rim too can be slightly moistened, if it starts to show signs of cracking (32-35). Continue only as long as you feel the walls are standing up under the pressure, then put it aside upside down on its rim to harden slightly, and start another base. Mary Rogers usually has 3 pieces on the go at once. As the form develops you may find the clay becomes too floppy to hold its shape, and a range of cups or plastic containers will be useful to stand these drying forms in, preferably with a flaring-out rim (36). Practise as many various ways as you can, moving outwards, or upwards, or inwards (this is collaring, gripping and gathering it in – just like 'slow throwing') (37-45). There is no one way of doing any of these methods, you discover so much for yourself and your experiments may lead you to very regular or to more amorphous forms.

Adding a foot

A pot must stand well. If your pot does not need a foot, you must prevent it from rocking by giving it a shallow depression under the base. But you may want to add a foot. A well-proportioned foot should not only allow the pot to stand properly, but should also balance the pot itself, and give a spring to the whole form. Adding clay is always best done before the clay hardens too much. If you add a coil to make the foot when the clay is really soft then you may be able to make it adhere just simply by smoothing it into the body. But usually if the pot has dried slightly then the best way is to make your foot separately, roughen up the surface on the pot (this is called 'keying'), apply some thick slip or 'slurry' to it (this is clay mixed with water to a creamy consistency (47)) and push the foot and pot together, smoothing them down with a modelling tool. Don't be in too much of a hurry to clear away the excess slip that squeezes out; let it set a little before you clean it away (48-54). When the pot is much drier the surface can be scraped smooth and the walls thinned. This is done

26

27

28

29

30

26/27/28/29/30 Adding sand. Use wet sand if the clay is slightly dry.

11

31 Take a ball of soft clay, shaping it between your hands. Insert your thumb gently.

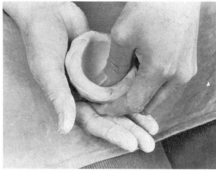

32 Continue pinching and stroking, turning the clay in your hand as you go.

33 You can make a rounder pot by pressing out a broad, wide base.

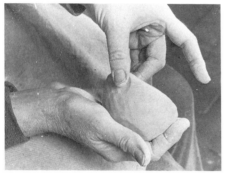

34 As you thin the walls by pinching, overlap each row of finger-marks with the next.

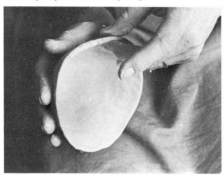

35 Continue pinching to thin the rim.

36 Rest your form upside down to stiffen; at the next stage, when it is more floppy, rest it in a container.

37 When slightly stiffer you can flare out the rim by easing the walls outwards.

38 Sections through the pot as it develops: see how the walls thin out.

39 To start a more conical shape, don't open out the pot so much with the thumb at first.

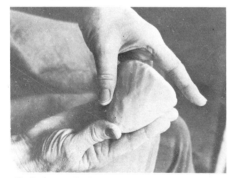

40 Squeeze the base gently around a finger, from the outside.

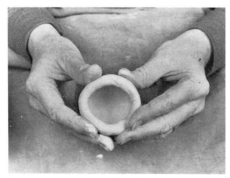

41 To start a more enclosed, egg-shaped form, ease the walls inwards.

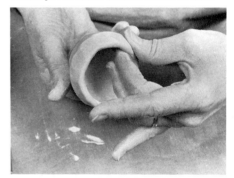

42 Leave a thick roll of clay at the top, pinching it inwards.

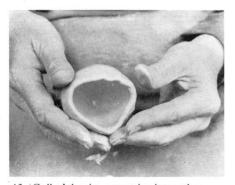

43 'Collar' the rim, squeezing it together, gathering it in and smoothing the wrinkles over.

44 Smooth out cracks all the while and close it in.

45 The finished pot, decorated and fired.

slowly and gently, using a scraper of some kind, (you can even choose one with a curve which fits the shape of your pot), either just past the leather-hard stage or when the pot is bone-dry for a very fine finish (wear a mask when doing the latter) (55). Or if you prefer, a rougher, thicker finish can be left. Many potters prefer their porcelain pots to be fine and delicate whereas earthenware or heavily grogged or textured stonewares are left robust and relatively heavy. But it is entirely up to you and how you respond to the clays you use (46). It is worth stressing that although you may begin with pinch pots it is not merely a beginners method. The control needed for just the use of hands and clay is infinitely subtle and some of the most beautiful pots ever made have been fashioned with the rhythmic movement of fingers and thumb in a small lump of clay held in the palm of the hand. Look at the masterpieces of Japanese asymmetrical balance, the tea bowls of the 17th century, to see what has been achieved in this simple way (415).

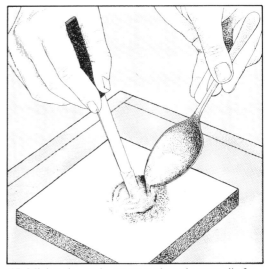

47 Mixing clay and water to make a slurry or slip for joining clay pieces together.

46 Oxidised stoneware pinch-pot by Sheila Fournier.

48 Choose the size: Mary Rogers keeps a selection of ring-shapes which she can use as guides to find a pleasing proportion for the foot.

Coiling

One of the limitations of pinching is size, for normally you are governed by what you can conveniently hold in a hand. Ladi Kwali, the famous Nigerian potter, overcomes this by using a large piece of clay which she punches into a hollow and then, moving round the form, she draws and strokes the walls up from inside with both hands; but this is only the start of her pot, for as this large 'pinch pot' hardens she adds coils to complete it; still gracefully walking round the pot, her movements take on the form of a slow, rhythmic dance (51, 52). Very varied shapes both in size and form can be made by adding one coil of clay on top of another and smoothing them together. You can add them to a flat base rolled or patted out (59, 60) or, like Mary Rogers does, onto a shallow pinched bowl. When she has pinched this base-bowl, Mary roughly shapes the coils in her hand as she feeds them on to the rim of her pot with a twisting motion (61, 62). But Ladi Kwali rolls the clay between her palms as she stands before her pot until the coil almost falls vertically downwards whereupon she catches it up again and continues rolling it between her hands until it is the right size and length to add to her rim. Each handbuilder seems to have some personal way with every method. However, the most common method of making coils is to roll a piece of clay on a slightly dampened surface, table top or board, with fingers and palms. Keeping the fingers slightly open and the arms free-moving with just a light touch you can make very long coils of clay, which again

49 Roll the clay out to an even thickness.

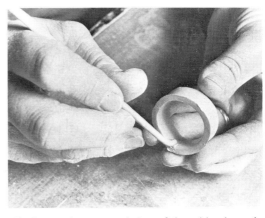

50 Cut out the measured piece of clay with ruler and knife, needle, or pin; cut a mitred seam and join with slurry and pressure from the fingers and tool.

51 Drawing up the clay.

52 Adding a coil to the top.

Ladi Kwali the Nigerian Potter making a large pinched and coiled pot; see also *427*.

53 Let the pot stiffen for a while before adding the foot. Mark the position of the base on the pot, then you can score and slurry both surfaces before joining. If you have a banding-wheel, it will help you see if the pot is centred on its foot.

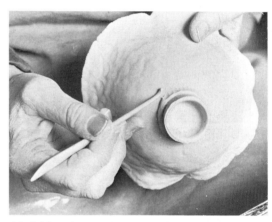

54 Add a coil to reinforce the join, on the inside and outside.

55 Scrape the surface to the required thinness and smoothness when it is dry. Porcelain is quite dry in up to 2 days. Mary uses a metal kidney with a similar curve to the pot.

should be soft and 'open' in texture. As the coils get longer and thinner move the hand over them, follow the coils as they expand outwards. Make several coils, keeping them damp under a moist cloth. Add one to the base and continue adding coils one on top of the other, separate ring upon ring (63).

To change direction, put the coil towards the inside of the rim if you want to go inwards or towards the outer edge if you want the pot to flare out, shaping, coaxing, and stopping only if the growing wall gets too floppy. A banding wheel, a kind of free-spinning wheelhead on a stand, is a great help in moving the form round and for seeing how the coiling is developing from all angles (64-73). The join of each separate coil and the coils themselves must be well knitted together both inside and outside the form (74). If the clay is soft and pleasantly textured this will be easy and some coilers use this natural joining movement to give a textural decoration to the surface either all over or in selected areas. Keep the edge even; if edges get too ragged they can either be cut off with a pin or beaten down before the next coil goes on; but keep the work flowing — don't worry so much about the silhouette as about your feeling for the

56 Completed form, glazed and fired by Mary Rogers.

57 Coiled pot by Elizabeth Raeburn

58 Coiled stoneware pot with sgraffito decoration by Helen Pincombe.

59 Pat or roll out a base, make coils with the fingers and palms.

60 Feed the first coil on, cut the joins in a mitre and press together.

61 You can use a pinch pot as a base for a smaller coiled pot – rest its curved base on a dry sponge.

62 Turn the pot round on the sponge as the coils are added. If you are pinching your coils, join them with a slightly spiralling motion.

63 Larger flat-based form, knit the coils together with your thumb.

growth of the form. Beating the sides with sticks – I use the rounded back of an old clothes-brush – stiffens up the form as well as giving a pleasing surface. The main thing is to feel the shape grow and grow under your hands.

Later, when harder, the surface can be treated in many ways, smoothed or roughened as you please or just left as you made it (57). Even the form itself can be changed by beating and rolling. Some hand-builders take a completed form – for example two half-spherical coiled shapes which have been joined together, or a coiled pot which has been completely closed-up – and by rolling or beating it change its shape (76-80). If you roll it over an uneven surface, you can also change the texture. (Remember to pierce the clay to let out the air!) Pots of enormous size and quite amazing variety of shape and texture are made by the coiling method (303, 318). They need not be symmetrical – and of course need not be pots at all, but organic forms or hollow sculptural objects. Since the late 40's coiling has enjoyed a revival among studio potters all over the world; international exhibitions always abound with coiled forms, large, small, delicate or robust (58).

64 Press the ends of each coil firmly together.

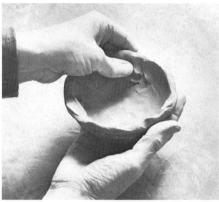

65 Smooth the inside surface – if you have pinched your coil, smooth in the opposite direction.

66 Knit the outside coils together, pushing down to the ridge below.

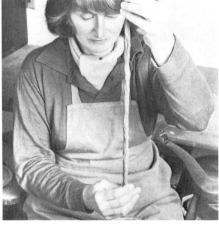

67 Mary Rogers makes a coil by twisting and squeezing vertically.

68 Place the coil towards the inside of the rim, to make an enclosed shape. You may need to leave it to stiffen for 2 hours or so if it gets floppy.

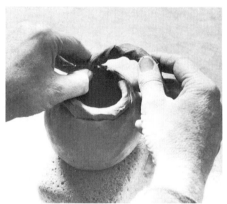

69 Close the mouth more and more.

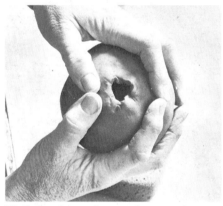

70 Collar the opening together smearing over the gathers.

71 Add a further coil to form a neck; use a stick or pencil to wrap it round.

72 Put a piece of paper with a hole in it to your lips and blow the form up; this can bulge out any irregularities in the form if the walls are thin enough and the pot still damp enough. Thrown bottles can be treated in this way too.

73 Completed fruit forms, decorated and fired, by Mary Rogers.

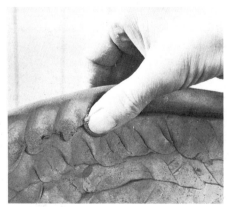

74 Remember, join the coils well.

16

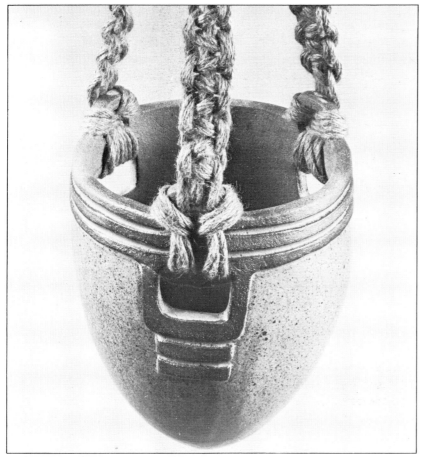

75 Stoneware plant pot, press-moulded base and coiled top, by Madeleine Cansfield.

Slab-building

This term is used to cover a wide variety of methods involving clay in different states of hardness: softer clay will need some support to allow it to stand; clay that has stiffened to a leather-hard condition will be able to stand easily on its own; or you can use clay states in between these two extremes.

Sheets of clay whether soft or harder can be made by patting out a lump by hand, or by rolling with rolling-pin or round stick. Either judge the thickness by eye or by using two even sticks within which the clay is rolled or beaten out (81). Slabs can also be cut from a large lump of clay singly, by using a wire harp that can be set to the required thickness (82), or you can use two notched sticks with a wire drawn taut across them which moves up one notch at a time to cut a whole mound of clay into slices of equal thickness (83). Once rolled or cut the slabs can be used soft or left to harden up.

If the clay is very soft you can use the 'wrap-around' method – you need a support in the shape of a rolling-pin or cardboard former such as a tube (319, 320): you wrap the clay around it, and then allow the clay to stiffen slightly before the support is removed. The virtue of using soft clay becomes apparent when joining the seams, as you can smooth them without the use of scoring or slipping. Bases can quickly be made of equally soft clay, cut out and joined on in a similar way. Because the clay in wrap-around forms is soft, all the joins are easily made, even if coils of clay have to be added inside them to make a smooth strong join between base and wall, and to add strength (84-95). It is a very free and comparatively spontaneous method of slabbing and of course the forms reflect this use of soft clay (368).

Once the clay has stiffened then much more hard-edged shapes like boxes with angles can be tackled. You should bevel the edges of the cut-out

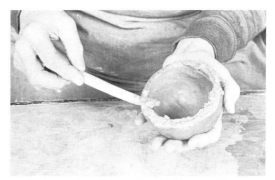

76 Make two hemispheres by pinching or coiling. Leave to stiffen by resting them on their rims. Then score and slurry the rims.

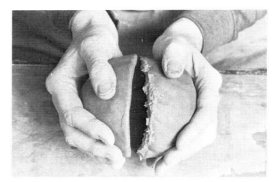

77 Push the two halves firmly together with a slight screwing motion.

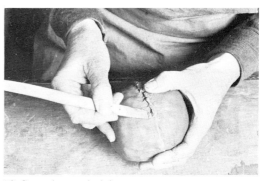

78 Smooth over the join.

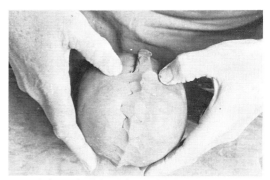

79 Reinforce the join with an added coil.

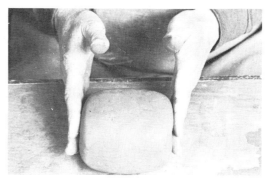

80 The hollow sphere – you can beat it into a variety of shapes, before you release the air by piercing it.

17

shapes to make a mitre joint, and score and slurry them liberally, before joining them together, rather as a wood-worker joins wood with glue. Stand the walls onto the base, so that as it shrinks it pulls the form together. Here again don't be in a hurry to clear away wet slip, let it stiffen and clean up a little later. Slab-work potters often use T- and set-squares, or cardboard or wooden templates to mark out the various parts of the slab pots they are making. In this way great precision can be achieved and shapes repeated over and over again (96-98). This slab method is

81 Roll out the clay between two sticks to make it an even thickness.

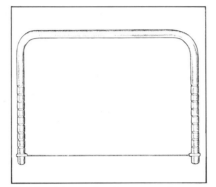

82 Metal harp showing taut wire and notches at regularly spaced intervals.

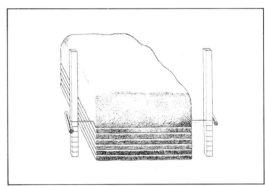

83 Method of slicing clay into sheets of equal thickness, wire moves up a notch at a time.

84 Measure and cut the rolled-out clay.

85 Mitre-cut the seams, slurry them.

86 Join inside and outside seams with pressure from a tool. Leave to stiffen a few hours.

87 Put the form on a rolled-out base, cut away the excess with a pin, leaving some over to smooth upwards with a tool.

88 Reinforce the inside join with a coil of soft clay.

91 Completed tree-lidded box by Mary Rogers. 2 pinholes show correct alignment for the lid.

89 A lid made in a similar way, flanged with a coil (use the base of the pot as a guide for size).

90 Push soft clay through the sieve to make 'leaves'. Remove with metal kidney.

used imaginatively by many handbuilders to make not only squared pots, like Ian Auld's monumental forms (*100*), but also ceramic sculpture like the lively boats, bridges and houses by Bryan Newman (*99*). You must experiment to find out which clay condition suits you best – the softer forms that come from quickly wrapping clay together, or the hard-edged, more precise shapes that come from clay allowed to stiffen so that you can handle it more slowly.

92 Pinch together the seam of the rolled out clay.

93 Cut away the excess with a pin.

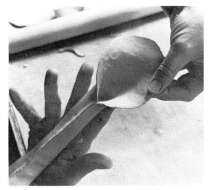

94 Flare out the opening.

95 The completed form painted in copper and fired, by Mary Rogers.

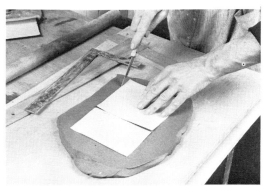

96 Cut around paper templates.

97 Mitre the edges, score and slurry the joints. Walls on top of base will obviate warpage and cracks.

98 Reinforce joins with a soft coil.

99 Slab-built bridge by Bryan Newman.

100 Slab-built stoneware pots with poured matt ash glazes by Ian Auld.

Tiles

The basic action of all these slabbing methods is to make a sheet of clay. As well as slab pots and sculpture you can simply leave the sheet flat and cut it into squares or other shapes to produce tiles. The main problem here is warping. Certain clays, especially if thin or uneven, will curl at the edges and distort badly during drying or firing. So the clay for tiles has to be of the right kind, and few potters actually make their own tiles these days. Ideally the clay should not only be the right composition, with a fairly high proportion of the non-plastic China clays and grogs (that is, fired, finely-ground clays), but should also contain the minimum of water, which can aggravate warping. So pressing tiles made from barely damp powdered clay bodies in specially constructed tile presses is the best way and the way they are all made industrially. But there is no reason why you cannot make your own tiles if you observe a few simple rules. Keep the dimensions as square as possible (if they are to be irregular shapes, beware, too many thin extensions will cause trouble unless the tile is quite thick). Keep the thickness absolutely even and not too thin,(depending on the size – e.g. a 6″ × 6″ tile could be about ½″ thick 15 × 15 × 1·3 cm), and do not have the clay too soft to start with.

There are various ways that the evenness of clay in thickness and regularity of shape can be achieved. There are tile cutters on the market that will actually do this for you. But you can set up tile frames with interlocking sticks (101), or just be very careful about your measurements, using set square and ruler, or template; roll out between two sticks of equal thickness. Some potters believe that cutting the tiles almost, but not completely through, so that the edges hold each other down as they dry, is a good tip to counteract warping – when almost dry they can be separated. But more usually, once pressed or rolled out, cut them to size and allow them to dry to a leather-hard state; then you must nurse them through the next drying stage, turning them over regularly on a completely flat, absorbent surface and finally perhaps stacking them so that their corners (the most vulnerable parts) are held as the tiles dry (102). If the clay is sandy or groggy to start with, and you are careful about the making and drying – and carry this care through to the firing stage as well, making sure the kiln shelves are flat, then you should be successful. Once you begin to master tile-making then not only larger or more ambitious shapes can be attempted but a whole range of decorative

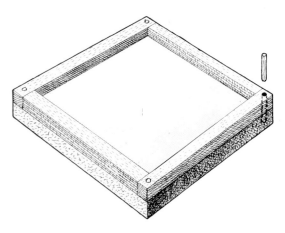

101 Roll out each tile in the wooden frame; a loose peg frees the interlocking sticks when the clay is firm.

102 Method of stacking tiles to prevent warping while drying.

103 Earthenware tile with added clay and incised decoration by Eileen Nisbet.

effects become possible, because tiles can not only be painted (*292*) but textured, or even quite heavily indented by pressing objects into them or rolling the clay out over prepared surfaces as you make them.

The higher the temperature to which you fire your tiles, of course, the more danger there is of distortion, and it is significant that the most prolific tile-makers in history have been the Islamic potters who covered their sacred buildings in lusciously coloured tiles of all shapes; they were all low-fired earthenware products (*104*). Eileen Nisbet has used some of these methods to produce her earthenware tile panel (*103*).

104 Persian tiles with overglaze painting, 12th century AD.

Press-moulding

Press-moulding is another way of using flat sheets of clay. Some potters believe that patting out the clay with the hands is the best method, because the particles of clay are properly aligned by the rhythmic beating, and they use this particular method to make the whole sheet of clay for a press-moulded dish. A beaten or evenly rolled-out sheet of clay, draped over or pushed into a 'former' made from absorbent material, will take that shape and, providing there are no undercut seams or edges, can easily be removed when it has reached a leather-hard condition. These formers, or 'moulds' as they are called, are usually made from grogged clay fired to biscuit temperature or from plaster of Paris, but any absorbent material will do. I have seen cardboard boxes lined with soft clay and when it stiffened the cardboard was cut away to reveal a clay box inside. To make a biscuit mould, you take a piece of well-wedged open-textured clay, liberally grogged or sanded bodies will do, and by a combination of beating, adding, scraping away and finally hollowing out, make the master shape you want (105). The mould, or rather two moulds (because you will end up with the possibility of putting the clay into the inside or over the outside of the mould), should be robust and with evenly-made sloping walls to make it easy to remove the shape when firm. Even if you only want one mould, you must hollow it out, because if it is left solid it may blow up in the kiln. It may take a long time but it must be thoroughly dry before it is fired slowly to biscuit temperature. Remember that any deviation of form or surface will be repeated every time you take a pressing from this master. So great care and accuracy is called for in making moulds: this is also true for the mould made in plaster, for in this case too the form is originally made in clay.

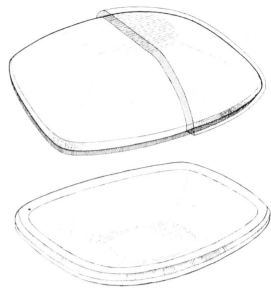

105 Clay mould.

There are two main reasons for using plaster of Paris: you can attempt a greater variety of shapes because the plaster doesn't have to be hollowed out and then fired, and the material is more absorbent. (Plaster has two disadvantages, in that if flakes of it get into clay they can blow up when fired leaving a hole, or worse, a shattered pot, so be careful and clean up well when using plaster of Paris anywhere in your workshop; and it is also more breakable than clay). Make the intended shape in clay, by making the solid shape upside-down on a flat board with – depending on the size of the work – an inch or two (2·5-5 cm) of space all the way round. Then cover it with plaster of Paris (buy the superfine quality). Opinions differ as to how this is done: some like the retaining walls, that hold the plaster of Paris in place while it sets, to be made of adjustable boards sealed with clay (106). This means that the liquid plaster is poured on to a depth of about an inch (2·5 cm) or so above the base of the clay. A flat-based but fairly heavy mould results. I have found one of the easiest ways is to cover the form in a smooth but not too thick plaster which is contained within a low wall round the clay form, then use thicker plaster, which you can scoop on with the hands, interleaved with long strips of scrim (a light bandage-like material). This method has the virtue of strengthening the mould and means that much less thick and therefore much lighter moulds result. A flattened base can easily be filed smooth when the plaster has set (107).

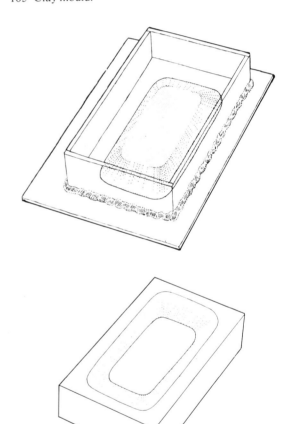

Plaster mould.

These methods give you a hollow plaster mould which you line with clay. You can also take another plaster mould from this one which you will be able to press clay *over*. You must stop the new plaster from sticking to the first mould by making the latter impervious, and this involves several coatings or washings of soft soap. But it is quite a long job, and perhaps the flop-over or hump-back mould is best made in clay. To do this you can either take a thick clay pressing from the plaster mould and fire that, or throw a thick shape on the wheel, cut and beat it into shape and mount it on a thrown stem (these are sometimes called mushroom moulds (108)).

Many formulae are given for mixing plaster (some will be found in the books in the Booklist) but I have always found that the best way is to sprinkle plaster gently *on* to the water (the amount will differ with the size of your mould). The plaster will build up on the surface of the water and will be absorbed by it if you gently shake your hand *below* the surface of

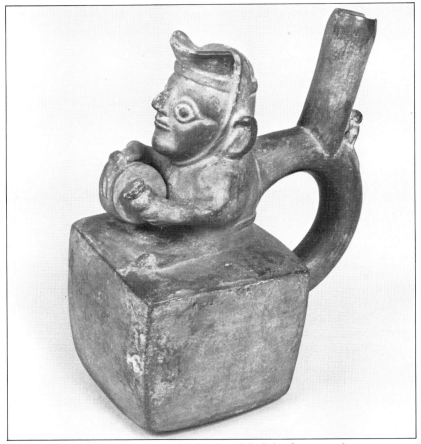

109 Pre-Columbian pot, press-moulded and modelled clay forms, earthenware, 8th century AD.

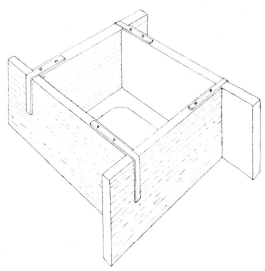

106 Making a plaster mould using interlocking boards as retaining walls.

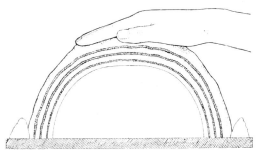

107 Making a plaster mould using layers of scrim.

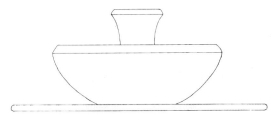

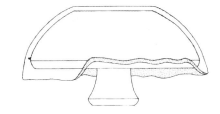

108 A 'mushroom' mould.

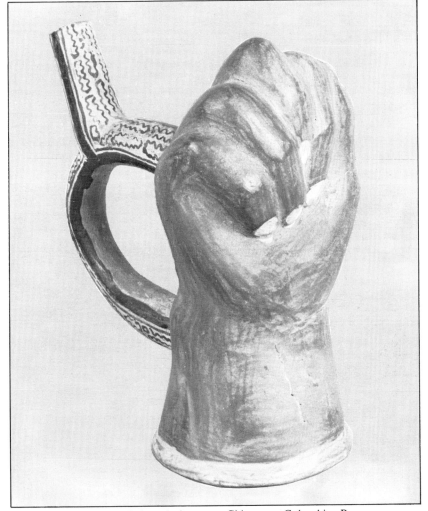

110 Press-moulded hand-shaped stirrup pot. Chimu, pre-Columbian Peru, 12th century AD.

the water (no bubbles will get in this way). Go on adding plaster until the water will not absorb any more. You can tell this has happened when the plaster pancakes on the surface, and will only dissolve very slowly even though you continue to agitate the water. You will now have to leave the creamy mixture for a few minutes, then pour away any thin film of water on top. Now act quickly but surely because the plaster will be setting fast. Pour and scoop it on to your clay master mould and *immediately* wash up all the plaster-covered bowls and tools – and your hands!

By pressing clay onto or into moulds like these all manner of forms, dishes and bowls of regular or irregular shapes, shallow or quite deep can be made. If done carefully, lifting the sheets of clay into or onto the mould is a simple matter. You can press the clay firmly onto biscuit or plaster with the help of a damp sponge, smoothing it completely home with a rubber kidney. You should generally take the pot out of its mould in a leather-hard state; this allows you both to smooth the edge and decorate the form if you wish.

Once you decide to use a support for the clay, then sheets of clay can be modified to include the use of pressed-in strips, pads or rolls of clay, allowing many decorative effects to be built in as you go. You can leave open spaces between your clay pieces, provided that the pot does not become so flimsy that the danger of violent distortion or collapse becomes probable (111-113). Clays of different types – so long as they are compatible – or a clay stained with different metal oxides (see p68 'Staining') can be pressed side by side together to give what is called 'solid agate', where the colour changes go all the way through like the name on Brighton rock (322-326). The one principle to remember in cases where solid sheets of clay are not used, is that even if the front of the piece is not smoothed over because some decorative effect or pattern is intended, the clay must be welded together on the back of the pressing. If this is not done the various strips and pads may all come apart. It is a good idea with this type of work which may, by its very nature, sometimes result in a kind of open lattice-work structure, to leave it in or on the supporting mould until it is quite dry. 'Laminated' or agate ware is best cleaned up with metal scrapers or kidney to reveal its true pattern when the clays are either very leathery or even dry.

By using two or more pressings together, with added bases and possibly necks, you can construct pots of all kinds. The pre-Columbian potters of South America used this method to make not only many of their pot forms, but the basic parts of many of their sculptural figures of animals and humans as well – limbs and detail were added afterwards (*109, 110, 365, 422, 423*).

Mix your Methods

Once your imagination has been stimulated there is literally no end to the handbuilding methods that can either be combined or invented afresh. For example, pinching and coiling go well together and coiled or thrown tops look fine on slabbed bases (*75*). Many bottles made by Hamada, the famous Japanese potter, are made in this way. Remember that clay is extremely versatile, it will respond to your touch if you keep in mind a few simple rules. Use soft clay, and squeeze and push pieces together also in a soft state. If you have to add slightly harder (leather-hard) pieces, then score the surfaces and add slip between them. Ease the pieces together carefully, pushing from the centre any air that might be trapped.

At every stage you can discover ways of using clay for yourself, no list of handbuilding methods could be exhaustive. I will only add two more

111 Add coils and other pieces over the mould.

112 Join the coils together with the fingers as for coiled pots, then beat down the surface to make a good bond.

113 Lift the clay away from the mould when it has stiffened to a leather-hard state.

114 Handbuilt head by Jill Crowley.

115 Modelled Raku goat by Rosemary Wren.

ideas to be experimented with; they have been used by many potters, each one adapting the method to produce a personal interpretation. They are both sculptural, the one using a certain amount of carving away whilst the other is based on modelling and building up.

Hollowed forms

With this method you simply take a lump of well-prepared clay and roll and beat it into a solid shape that pleases you. It can be smooth, textured, or both, you decide. Once the outside shape is decided upon then you must turn your attention to the inside and hollow out the form. This is done with a loop-ended turning tool, or piece of stiff wire twisted into a claw or loop and mounted on a stick, or even a sharp spoon if the clay is soft. It is best to mark the thickness of the edge all the way round at the top of the form to give yourself something to aim at. You can start taking away the clay from inside almost as soon as you have finished shaping, but the thinner the walls become the more you will have to wait to scoop out more clay and smooth down the inside. The edge can be completed with damp chamois leather or of course a coil added to give a positive finish.

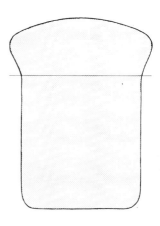

116 Hollowing out a solid form.

This method is particularly good for making lidded forms, because the original shaping produces lid and body all at the same time, the line from one to the other being unbroken (116). To make the lid you just slice a good thick section off the top with a wire once the form is shaped, leave the clay to stiffen up, then start to hollow out base and lid, frequently bringing them back together to keep their shape. Some time before the clay gets too hard some locking device to keep the lid on is needed. A flange can be added in the form of a coil on either lid or base or simply three small balls of clay welded on round the lid's inner edge will suffice (117). I have seen beautiful lidded pots made in this way, some resembling organic, almost fungoid forms, others looking more like bones. The lid and body really make one complete form, and if a virtue is made of the fact that the solid form before hollowing is treatable in so many different ways – beating, scoring, burnishing – then exciting possibilities open up for the handbuilder.

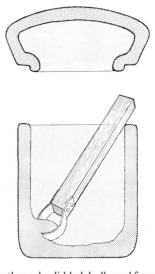

117 Section through a lidded, hollowed form, showing flange.

120

121

118 Modelled horse, T'ang dynasty China,
618-906 AD.

119 Medieval musicians, modelled stoneware, by Maggie Humphrey. Costumes and instruments from original sources such as Bosch and Breughel.

122 Covered pot, oxidised stoneware with modelled added clay decoration by Ian Godfrey.

Modelling

If clay is to be dried and fired easily and successfully it cannot be too thick in any one section. For this reason the kind of clay modelling that potters have done from the earliest times has always differed from the sculptor's use of clay which quite often is then cast into another material like metal. Models that are made up from rolls and balls and rope-like shapes made in the hand, small-scale, seem to suit the potter's clays best (*17*). I think of Greek horses sitting on the top of shallow-lidded pots, or the little bird knob handles so beloved of the Chinese potters (*411*). The tree on Mary Rogers' tree-lidded box was modelled and then added on. (The 'leaves' were made by pushing clay through a sieve – this also makes good lion's manes or hair – and it can be finished off with other tools (*90, 91*)). Children seem instinctively to have the right scale for pottery modelling with their dinosaurs and coiled snakes (123).

The rules, if there are any hard and fast ones, are simple: keep the clay open – sandy, groggy; don't let any section of the model get too thick; add pieces when soft if possible, or if harder then well-scored and slipped; generally avoid very thin or spiky pieces or sudden changes from thick to thin. If you must model thick pieces, as thick as a fist, for example, then you must remember to hollow out the inside, or the model will explode in the kiln. But clay is such a versatile medium that I hesitate to lay down any controls because once you know your clay and how it behaves both in the making and firing, there is no limit to what you can make. Certainly today many younger potters have taken to clay modelling as their way of expression. Look at the work of Ian Godfrey (*122*), Jill Crowley (*114*) and Rosemary Wren (*115*), or in a more illustrative way Maggie Humphrey (*119-121*), to see what can be done once you know your material.

123 Modelled monsters by Simon Keeler and Ben Casson (7 and 8 years).

Throwing

Tomb paintings and statuettes (*124*), date the discovery of the potter's wheel from about 5000 years ago somewhere in the Middle East: its advent meant not only a far greater output of pottery generally – the wheel is a much faster way of working – but a different sense of form and a different range of shapes came with its immediacy and dynamic force. Once invented, the wheel spread rapidly and took different forms. The potter's wheel is essentially a flat turntable mounted on top of a shaft; but how that shaft was fixed to allow it to rotate, and what kind of power was applied to it, differed widely. 'Continental' and geared kick-wheels developed in Europe; in Japan the potter still sits cross-legged at his hand-wheel (*125*).

The potter ceased to provide his own power when first the 'slave' or 'boy' wheel came in: here someone else gives the power by turning a handle on a system of belts that move the shaft. Later the electrically-driven power wheel brought this principle to completion, and although there are now several quite different types on the market all electric wheels should conform to certain requirements if they are to be considered successful

124 Carved limestone statuette of early Egyptian thrower and his wheel. Old Kingdom 2700 BC.

125 Hamada seated at his wheel, he uses a stick to turn it.

by the potter: they must have a range of speeds from slow to fast, without losing 'torque' – the ability to withstand a heavy pressure downwards and inwards on to the moving wheel-head; they must be smooth and quiet in operation, characteristics they should share with the simpler kick-wheels; comfort too is a factor common to all wheels. Whether you stand or sit at your wheel will probably have something to do with how long you like to throw at any one session, but, whichever you choose, a well designed wheel will not make you hunched or distorted over the wheelhead. There are many pitfalls in buying a wheel and it is wise to seek advice from a professional potter (when not too busy!) who uses one day in and day out, before paying from between £100+ (for some kick wheels) to £350+ (for the more expensive electric models). Once you have bought it, maintain it, get used to taking the wheel-head off at the end of the day, oil it to the manufacturer's instructions, make sure that the centre hole in the tray doesn't allow clay to pass through and onto the spindle carrying the wheelhead. All these wheels have a different feel to them; but basically the main difference between a hand- or kick-wheel and a power-assisted wheel is that the former gives a direct, immediate and therefore, infinitely subtle communication between body and brain, whereas the power-wheel has speed and accuracy and gives the potter the ability to handle large amounts of clay with comparative ease. Good pots can be made on either.

126 Natural sponge.

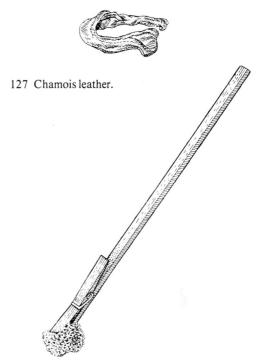

127 Chamois leather.

The thrower's tools

The tools that throwers use become after a while a collection of highly personal aids to shaping clay on the wheel, but there are several that can be found near to hand at almost every wheel.

Sponge

Apart from the general cleaning up sponge, which can be synthetic, potters use *natural sponges* when throwing. Some potters like to use the sponge to carry water from the waterpot to the hands so that a steady stream can be squeezed over the hands and thence evenly over the spinning clay (209). Natural sponges are much kinder on the hands as well as seeming to pick up more water: my own choice for throwing would be a flat, open textured sponge that easily slips into the bottoms of bowls and mops up without distorting the clay in any way (126). Potters seldom throw with the sponge, because it tends to wash away the clay, and leave the rough sandy particles standing proud; some smooth porcelains may be an exception. But a sponge is needed for mopping up water from inside the pot – sometimes they are mounted on sticks so that the inside bases of tall shapes can be cleaned without distortion (128). The edges of rims are often thrown with a fine piece of *chamois leather* that presses back the gritty particles and gives a very smooth rim (127, 218).

128 Sponge on a stick.

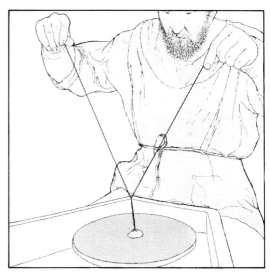

129 Twisting two strands of wire together.

Wire

A *wire* to cut the finished pot from the wheel-head is essential. You can buy twisted wire, or you can twist the plain wire by hand (129), on the wheel or even in a metalworker's brace holding the two strands in the jaws of the chuck while the other ends are held in a hook on the wall. Wires should be secured at either end by a toggle, pieces of wood or the like, to prevent snagging or kinking that will quickly cause fraying (130). Most potters prefer twisted steel wire because it seems to release the pot in the most positive way as well as giving a pleasant pattern underneath pots that are not going to be turned or finished in any other way. The shell-like spiral mark so beloved of Bernard Leach is achieved by slowly rotating the pot as the wire is pulled through, but other patterns can be made with different movements. The secret of all good wiring-off is a taut

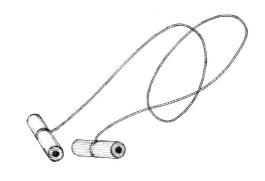

130 Twisted wire with toggle ends.

wire held flat to the wheel-head – and here the toggles are useful as grips (154). Timing too is important, and it is best to cut through as soon as you can after throwing, especially in flat ware, even if the pot is not going to be lifted away from the wheel-head or bat immediately. The longer you leave it, the riskier wiring-through becomes, and there is nothing as depressing as seeing the wire ride up and slice off the base of the pot just at the moment of triumph when it seems so proudly finished.

Bats

Many potters throw not on the wheel-head itself but on a kind of false head that can be lifted off the wheel-head carrying the pot with it. The advantages are obvious: no distortion of the pot on top from lifting it off, therefore more ambitious shapes may be made; the pot may be brought back, re-centred easily and more work done on the pot if necessary – for example another piece added on. These bats are made (or you can make them yourself) from a variety of materials such as hard asbestos, resin-bonded ply, slate, plaster of Paris or even softer materials (if well supported) like compressed board. The harder the material the more durable, but the more difficult to cut, whereas the softer materials, easier to cut, damage more easily. The fixing methods differ greatly. Some potters simply throw a ridged pad of stiffish clay, slightly damp it, and bang the bat down on this (131, 132). Others again have studs drilled or brazed on to the wheel-head and corresponding holes cut in all the bats (133). Others yet again keep square bats (all the aforementioned would be round) but mount 4 semicircular pieces on the edge of the head with a square in the middle to take the bats. Once set up, a bat system does make the completion of pots easier, especially bowls and plates and other flat ware that tends to distort (and often stays distorted) if lifted off.

Trimming tools

Potters use a *pin mounted on a stick* for cutting away waste or uneven clay at the top of a pot (215) – throwing so that this is necessary is not a practice to be cultivated but, like the occasional pricking of air bubbles, the use of the pin to correct a mistake is sometimes unavoidable for even the best of potters. A *bamboo stick* about 6″-9″ (15-23 cm) long with angled end and bevelled cutting edge is useful for clearing away unwanted clay at the base of the pot just prior to cutting through with the wire.

Ribs

Ribs can be made of any hard material, wood, slate, metal, leather, bone (134). Some potters do not use these at all but it is significant that the professional potters I know, as well as all the peasant communities of potters one can still find, do use ribs of some form or another. They are useful to clear away slurry from the pot before lifting it off (248), but are of most use in compressing the clay during the throwing. In this way a rib enables the potter to get much thinner walls – and therefore larger pots for the amount of clay used, and more articulated shapes (184, 185). By using the pressure of the rib on the outside and supporting the pot with the fingers of the hand on the inside wall, the clay form can be changed in a very positive way. Hamada uses all kinds of ribs, often on the inside of bowls, to give him just the right strength of curve at a particular point (152). It is not throwing with a former, in no sense is the clay pushed up to a predetermined silhouette. It is sometimes claimed that a rib has a deadening effect, and if this is so, then the rib has been used in the wrong way, more like a turning-tool on the surface, than what it should be, a firmer extension of the thrower's hand. To see Isaac Button, or any of the great country potters, lift and swell out a form with his wooden rib would show immediately how the rib gives you more power and more selection of form.

131 Throw a flat disc of stiff clay, groove it with a rib or turning tool.

132 Damp the clay and thump down a bat squarely and firmly on top.

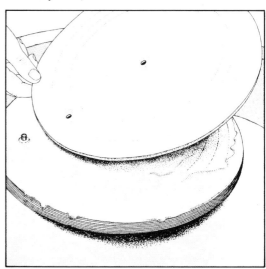
133 Method of fixing a bat; holes correspond to studs on the wheel-head.

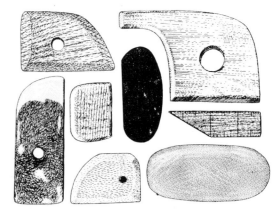
134 A variety of ribs in wood, metal, rubber and slate.

Measuring devices

Potters use widely differing methods for measuring their pots, whether for lid sizes, or to check the repetition sizes of pots that have to match each other. You can use *callipers* (135, 202) and *rulers* (I recommend wooden callipers – or even plastic ones with a butterfly bolt – but not metal because they soon go stiff with clay and oil on the calliper's pin and then become almost immovable), *sticks* with notched marks for the various measurements, even elaborate *cross-like constructions* with a third arm pointing down, so that when offered into a bowl it will give the width and depth at the same time. You can make or buy adjustable throwing gauges; these have a pointer that can be pre-set to give the height and width of the pot to be made. They usually clamp onto the wheel or tray at a convenient place just out of range of moving hands (136).

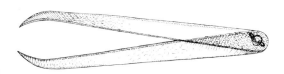

135 Callipers.

Turning tools

A very large range indeed is available from potters' suppliers but most potters make use of only two or three, if that. They are usually made from metal, and fall roughly into two types: those that *gouge out the clay*, and are therefore of wire or thinner strap metal in a loop shape; and those that *cut the clay away*, and are made of flat metal bent at an angle, and have a cutting edge that must be kept really sharp at all times. This type is easy to make out of mild steel (137). Both types come in many shapes and sizes. They should all fit the hand comfortably because they must be held firmly against the spinning clay (166-172).

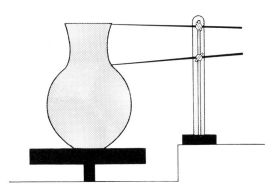

Clay bodies for throwing

It is a maxim shared by craftsmen of very different kinds that it is sensible to expect from your materials only what they can give naturally and without strain. This is nowhere more true than when considering the clays and minerals that go to make up the bodies that we potters use. You can buy from potters' merchants many mixtures suitable for throwing that will give a variety of finished colours; or the more experienced potter can buy the various pulverised clays and feldspars, quartz and sand that go to make up a body. Here, though, you need to know what you are doing and at least one item of equipment is almost essential – either a dough-mixer or blunger (these mix the ingredients together), or a pug (to chop up the moistened materials, then squeeze them together through a tapered extrusion barrel). Whether you buy it ready mixed or make it yourself you still have to test the body to find out what it will do – not impose your will on it. Some clays have a positively benign nature, will throw thick or thin, large or small, without warping or distorting; these will allow the thrower the choice as to whether the forms will be turned, or simply thrown directly so that every ounce of clay goes into the form, needing only the wire to separate it from the wheel-head. Such versatile clays are rare and are usually the outcome of much trial and error on the part of the professional potters earning their livings by their craft, usually using highly plastic ball clays. Most clays bought from the potters' suppliers will not meet these conditions; many of them will be expected to serve a much wider range of activities; but a number of them are perfectly usable clays once their limitations are accepted.

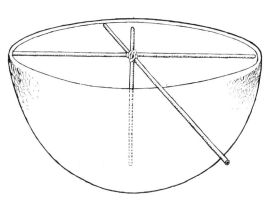

136 Measuring devices for width and depth.

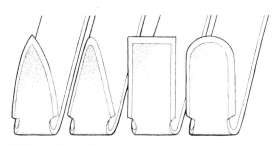

137 Angle turning-tools.

'Suitable for throwing on the wheel or for handbuilding processes, will fire well in any atmosphere with a temperature range of 900°C-1280°C.' This is a typical quotation from a supplier's catalogue; somewhere in that description is a clay that can be used, but it tries to be all clays to all potters. So the buyer must learn to interpret. Enquire and get samples where possible. Find out if the bodies are based upon ball clays – usually more plastic than the tight, fine-ground Midland fireclays so often used by Stoke-on-Trent suppliers. These fireclays have many good properties,

138 Bowls thrown with a pound of clay to the same size will increase your throwing skill and awareness of form.

but ease of throwing is not one of them; they make good 'throwing-and-turning' bodies. The information you need is:

Temperature
Will the body supplied fire to the temperature you require for your kiln and your glazes?

Throwing
Try throwing weighed-out lumps to determine how well it throws; does it need turning because it refuses to pull up into its full potential height or width?

Warping and shrinkage
These can be tested and measured by throwing carefully documented shapes and observing the clay's behaviour after the biscuit and glaze firings.

Final colours, glaze fit
Lastly, do you like the colour of the fired body? Do your glazes look well over it – more to the point do they fit well over it, or do you have excessive crazing or worse?

All these have to be considered; as well as what may be the most important point of all: reliability of consistency. Having got a clay body that you are reasonably satisfied with, will the supplier keep up his standards? All you can do here is send back the bad batch (don't give in), and send your praises and thanks when he does deliver good clays time after time.

Altering clay bodies for throwing
There are a number of things you can do to improve ready-made clay bodies. Firstly, many of the ultra-smooth ones will be improved by the addition of a little – say 8%-10% – of a fine clean silica sand, or try adding 25% of a good plastic ball clay; wedge it to the same consistency as the body supplied, and then wedge and knead it in (26-30). Both these additions are to help the clay to throw well but all the tests above must still apply because vitrification may have been altered. In the same way the blending of bought clays may improve colour and possibly the way the body throws, but it may bring other disadvantages, so you must still go through all the tests for shrinkage, glaze fit etc. It is a fascinating quest, and professional potters just as much as the beginner are always concerned with the search for the perfect clay body for their needs.

The condition of clay for throwing
Probably the one thing that the would-be thrower can control is the softness or hardness of the clay when he goes to the wheel to throw. This may alter as experience builds up or it may need to be different for the job in hand, e.g. flat plate or tall bottle. I would advocate that the beginner accept the limitations that softer clay implies, i.e. simpler shapes and thicker-walled pots, because the centring, opening and shaping processes will concern you most at these early stages. So use very soft clay and easy hand movements will follow. Flat ware incidentally, plates, flatter dishes and bowls, need never be made with harder clay, because they are by definition objects with little vertical form, and rely heavily on turning to finish them off. As skill and confidence mount you can try using stiffer clay, but there are many experienced potters who still use very soft clays for throwing. The slightly harder – never stiff – clay body seems to be reserved by most potters for very direct throwing, when no turning is intended, and also for functional vessels such as jugs and teapots that will later hold liquid, and therefore have to be light to pick up and use. This is because harder clays often allow you to throw thinner walls, but they are more difficult for the beginner to handle.

139 Damp the bat, firmly thump down the lump of soft throwing clay.

140 *Centring grips:* i equal pressure with both hands.

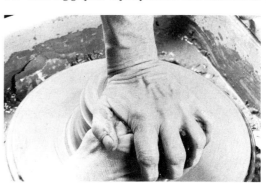
141 *Centring grips:* ii left arm vertical above clay.

142 *Centring grips:* iii right wrist gripped firmly by left hand gives extra pressure.

143 *Centring grips:* iv one hand on the other. Right hand thumb helps to keep clay in.

You can practise more easily and develop your skills more quickly if you weigh out each piece of clay before throwing. Although all the different clays we have mentioned will give slightly different results, especially depending on how soft or hard they are, there are nevertheless certain rough guidelines in the weights and subsequent sizes thrown. For example, a 1 lb (0·5 kilo) ball of clay should give you a bowl approximately 6″ wide × 3″ deep (15 cm × 7 cm) and a cylinder 5″ high × 4″ wide (13 cm × 10 cm) throwing with an average earthenware or stoneware body. Remember to keep notes which record the information you find out for yourself, so that you can check progress and build up experience (138). See chart on p.81-83 (366).

144 Opening centred lump of clay: with one finger, helped by other hand.

Centring

When you finally get to the wheel with your soft clay, bring with you the right frame of mind as well. Throwing should be fun even to begin with, and then give a deep pleasure as your control and range develop. But if the element of play is to lead on to a more serious study, then you will need concentration and discipline. The wheel itself works by the turning of a shaft that produces centrifugal force at the wheel-head. In effect this means that everything put on the wheel, clay, water, is spun off towards the edge. Using but containing this force allows the potter to throw shapes. It is also why, of the two basic shapes, the bowl is physically the easier to make for most beginners. It is outward going in the way that the wheel wants all shapes to go.

145 Opening centred lump of clay: with all fingers, helped by other hand.

Before tackling either shape, however, the thrower must get the clay in the middle of the wheel-head. Centring is rightly considered difficult by beginners, but as I shall never tire of saying, much heartbreak could be avoided by having well-prepared soft clay to begin with. The wheel-head should be slightly damp, the ball or cone of clay should be brought down firmly (but not necessarily thrown down) on to the centre. The wheel is spun fast in an anti-clockwise direction and from now on it's practice plus close observation and a willingness to try different hand positions. What the hands are doing, whilst taking enough water to lubricate the clay, is bringing pressure inwards and downwards in order to bring the clay to the centre. Avoid quick, jerky movements in throwing; movements must flow. The inward pressure of the hands will bring the clay up into a column or cone, the downward force will flatten it out (be careful not to trap air in the top of the cone); these two movements must blend until the thrower feels (not necessarily sees) that the clay is in the centre (139-143).

146 Opening centred lump of clay: use thumb only, clay cradled in hands.

Bowl and cylinder

The two main shapes in throwing are the bowl and the cylinder, and all other shapes are based on these two forms. Once centred you must decide on one or other of them: the first movement of your fingers determines the shape to come. Most bowls start with a concave-shaped base, either narrow or wide depending upon the conception of the form (144-155). All cylinders start with a flat base, test the thickness with a pin, it should be roughly the same as the finished walls at the base of the pot (156-161). There is no one way of holding the hands to produce any shape, but generally speaking it is sensible to realise certain basic principles:

147 Opening out, come up and out, slow down the wheel the wider the pot gets.

1 Throwing is a two-handed business, so link the hands by steadying one with the thumb or fingers of the other (some potters rest their arms on the edge of the wheel-tray); with much larger pots brace your right elbow into the body and see if that helps too.

148 Repeat the action moving hands from base to rim.

149 Change grip, left hand inside, right hand outside, join the hands for steady grip.

150 Move upwards slowly but with a fluid movement – keep hands linked.

151 A method of firming the rim.

152 To remove the slurry, move the rib or kidney gently from the rim in to the middle – this smoothes out any ridges but retains visual spiral of throwing process.

153 Make a bevel with a turning tool or bamboo tool at the base for the wire to pass underneath the pot.

154 Hold the wire taut and flat to the bat – turn the wheel slowly if you want a shell pattern underneath.

2 The pressure of the hands is *strong* to begin with and the wheel speed is *fast*. As the throwing progresses both the hand and finger pressures, as well as the speed of the wheel, get *gentler*.

3 Clay at the base of the walls of a pot is wasted – the excess has to be turned away. Try to get the clay up from the bottom. A pot grows from its roots, not by thinning out only the top third of the form. Indeed I believe that the rim of a pot should be kept sturdy while the throwing progresses, even if it is to be thinned out later on.

4 With a bowl shape you simply contain the clay to stop it from going out too far; the *inside* curve is vital to the whole form.

5 With a cylinder you are controlling the clay by stopping its natural inclination to move outwards. 'Collaring', i.e. encircling the cylinder within your two hands and moving with a fairly fast wheel from the base of the form up to the top, may be a great help in gaining height. 'Pulling up' is when the left hand is inside the pot: the inside (left) hand is placed slightly above the outside (right) hand and it is at this pressure point, where the clay is almost bent between the two pressures (for example fingers or knuckles) that the clay is lifted and the cylinder moves up and up; linking hands here when you can is a help.

6 In the West we use the anti-clockwise motion of the wheel so that the hands work somewhere between 4 and 6 o'clock, supposing the wheel-head were a clock face. In this way the clay comes into and passes through the hands.

155 Paper over the wet rim can help to lift off a wet bowl form: the air sealed inside keeps the shape stable.

156 Open the centred lump to form a flat base, all the rest of the clay comes to the side ready to be pulled up.

157 Thumb and fingers helped by the other hand make the first pull upwards.

158 Left hand inside, fingers just above fingers of outside right hand, making a step, link hands and lift up as the wheel spins quickly.

159 Keep this grip up to the top.

160 Use a rib to clear away slurry and to straighten and compress the wall.

161 Dry the hands, wire under the base of the pot and lift off.

Practise! Cut the shapes in half with a wire to check the thickness of the walls – a very slight taper from thicker base to thinner top is ideal but edges can be thickened for strength (162-164). The used clay can be wedged and kneaded and used again and again. It might get tired or over-used but fresh clay can be added, and if you allow several days for it to pick up again it will be as good as new. So nothing is wasted and you are gaining experience all the time.

Turning

Turning is sometimes a necessity, for instance when a bowl or dish shape made in soft clay will not stand up during the throwing unless it is left thick at the base; and sometimes it is an aesthetic choice. Potters differentiate between 'skimming', which is little more than tidying up the base edge, and full turning, involving a foot for the pot to stand on. Usually the procedure is to allow the form to dry to a cheese-hardness, turn it upside down on the wheel, get the pot on centre and hold it down. Some potters, such as David Leach, just damp the rim and the wheel-head, tap the pot into the middle and with one finger on the centre of the base, pare away the clay with a sharp turning tool. Beginners would be well-advised to hold the pot down with carefully rolled firm pieces, or a complete ring, of softish clay gently pressed on to the side of the pot and on to the wheel-head. Many potters work with the wheel head covered with a sheet of firm clay that grips the rim of the pot to be turned. Potters talk endlessly about the 'foot-ring' that is the foot on which the pot stands. It is of great concern to them that the foot and rim relate to each other. Try to make them look as if they belong together. The turning will give a different texture to the throwing; the width and depth of the foot, and the visible track that the turning tool makes as it moves across the

162 A section through a bowl that does not need a turned foot-ring.

163 An upright bowl designed to have a turned foot ring.

164 Section through showing amount to be turned away.

35

clay, all these must work together aesthetically and serve the demands of function in a successful piece of turning (165-172).

Planning is essential if the potter has turning in mind. It is not something that you should resort to reluctantly after the form has been made because it is too heavy or the shape unsatisfactory. It can be a creative act in the hands of a skilful potter. To see Hamada use his turning tool to pare away swathes of sandy clay from around the base and under the foot of the pot is to witness an artist craftsman at work to whom the turning is absolutely as important as the throwing was earlier on. The two form an inseparable part of the whole. When the thrower knows he is going to finish by turning then from the very moment he opens the ball of clay on the wheel the depth, width, thickness of wall must all be borne in mind and held at certain stages because turning will complete the form later. The experienced potter sees the rim, walls, belly, foot and the cut of the foot-ring all completed in his mind's eye, the hands unerringly carry through the process to the end. Generally speaking there is a generosity of depth and cut of form about all good turning that speaks of right concept; and this is as true of small delicate pots in smooth porcelain as it is of great rugged-clayed stonewares. If the turning is mean or skimpy it really is not worth doing it in the first place (*289, 291, 301, 302, 370*).

Further throwing practice

After practising the two basic shapes the thrower can try a whole range of other forms. **Flat or shallow plates** are made by using a movement like the one that flattens out the cylinder's base, and it is as well to compress the clay of this flat disc by extra pressure of the fingers or even by passing

165 Wipe the rim with a damp sponge (the concentric rings on the bat help to centre it), tap it firmly down when on the middle and keep one or two fingers firmly pressed onto the base while turning the outside.

166 Steady the pot and press down three lumps of rolled clay to hold it firmly. The hands are linked, arm rested, tool held firmly as you begin to turn the clay from the side of the foot.

167 Clear the clay away from the inside – one hand steadies the other.

168 Turning on a bed of stiff clay – a cutaway portion allows for a lip of bowl or jug.

169 Turn *over* a 'chuck' made with a rounded thick rim onto which you press the bowl.

170 Feel the thickness of the wall and judge how much more to turn away.

171 Turn with the pot placed *inside* the chuck and tapped firmly in to hold. Bottle and rounded forms are usually turned in this way.

172 A firm dome of clay the same diameter as the pot makes a good chuck.

a rib firmly over the surface; this will help to prevent cracking. All flatter shapes, of course, must be adequately supported by using a larger bat or wheel-head to throw on. There are two main methods of tackling the rim of flat plates and dishes. Either the clay is thrown outwards in a horizontal movement all the way, and the edge becomes a thinned-out extension of this movement, or the edge is thrown up more vertically as in a cylinder, and then slowly bent over outwards to form the horizontal rim. Both ways need good control and a slow, smooth wheel movement (173-179). Plates, dishes and bowls, in fact all forms that should have a sweeping unbroken line, often benefit from the potter moving the fingers or ribs from the outer edge back into the centre spot as the wheel spins slowly. In this way the slow flattened spiral that results will give a very satisfying finish to the work. If the plate is to be turned then, to prevent sagging in firing, many potters turn either a double foot-ring, one at the edge, another part way into the centre, or they leave a little stud of clay at the centre just a little bit shallower than the outer foot-ring (180).

At this point the thrower can consider the **spherical form**, which might grow from the rounded base of a bowl, in which case it will probably need turning in a 'chuck' (a thick, short clay cylinder which you make to hold the pot in, upside down (171)), or from the flat base of a cylinder. This is the fascination of throwing – the way the forms merge to give a subtle range of shapes. I feel that the main dilemma about the sphere is when to start making the actual belly of the pot. If the rounded form is started too early on in the throwing process, say after the first pull upwards, then too squat a shape may be formed, increasing the possibility of collapse a little later on. On the other hand, to expect too tall or finished a cylinder to turn

173 Both hands move the clay downwards and outwards, use soft clay and slowish wheel.

174 Use a pin to gauge the thickness, it's very easy to get the bases of flat ware too thin, especially near the centre.

175 Gather up the clay to form the rim.

176 Move the rib or kidney over the surface to get a sweeping line. The other hand supports the rim.

177 Another way of throwing a large plate: throw a flat base with all the surplus clay moved to the side to form a short cylinder.

178 Bend the cylinder wall outwards with a slow-moving wheel.

179 Settle the wide rim with a rib, support the clay underneath with the other hand – very slow wheel speed.

180 On small plates, you need often turn only one supporting stud in the middle, large ones often need a double foot-ring to stop sagging.

into a sphere is to invite such a thin-walled form that it will probably split its sides before it can dry out. I think therefore a thickish-walled cylinder with well closed-in top rim is the ideal. Then the inside hand can reach right down to the base (any distortion at the rim can be corrected each time the hand reaches the top again), push firmly upwards and outwards supported only by the outside finger – holding a rib or not as you wish – and then those outside fingers will take over, as you round the belly and the wheel quickens as you aim for the smaller opening at the top. This change of emphasis, inside hand to outside hand, must be a flowing movement, a swelling – then a gathering in, slow to quick. The clay will probably only allow you to make two such movements before it becomes too extended (181-184). Spherical forms are some of the most beautiful but the most exacting forms to throw (*356, 372, colour 16, back cover 1*).

By the use of the rib softer shapes can be turned into more angular, articulated ones. The rib held in the outside hand can bring pressure to bear on the inside fingers that support the clay to give a strong almost horizontal turn to a pot and give great strength and clarity of line to neck and rim, side wall and shoulder (185, 186).

181 Keep the top in after every pull – 'collaring'.

182 Swell out the form, knuckle opposite inside finger tips.

183 Quicken the wheel and move inwards, outside hand doing most of the work.

184 The rib will allow an even thinner wall and a larger form; use it to clear away the slurry that sometimes makes a wet form sag.

185 The rib can give a rounded form a sharper angle and marks lines that accentuate the change of form at shoulder or neck.

186 Use the rib to firm an upright rim.

Throwing larger pieces

Given a good clay, sturdy wheel and above all the will to try, much larger forms can be tackled as the skill of the thrower develops (187-190). Some shapes lend themselves to large, single-piece throwing, as they stand well on their own. The broad-based medieval pitcher form, tapering towards the top, is just right for the large lump of clay, centred, opened to a wide base and then pulled upwards into what is essentially a truncated cone shape, that stands as firm as a milk churn (192-195, *191*). Providing the thrower does not tackle too much too soon this type of form will give good jugs, vases, store jars etc., and later the sides can be bellied and the top collared in to increase the range (*420*).

But larger still? Yes, it certainly is possible; once we recognise that certain sizes or forms are not possible with one piece of clay, then there are ways and means to achieve really large pots. Potters from all civilisations have thrown pots in more than one stage by one way or another. Sometimes, as in Japan, because the clay was so difficult to use, even small bottles were made by adding a coil round the top of the slightly

187 Lift the rudimentary cylinder with a collaring action.

188 For a larger piece of clay use a knuckle on the outside.

189 The inside fingers are just above the outside knuckle to pull up a 'step' of clay.

190 The rib removes slurry, straightens the form and if you wish will either remove or flatten out throwing ridges depending on the pressure you exert.

191 English Medieval jug, dusted-on copper and raw galena glaze.

stiffened, bellied form, and then the neck thrown on. At other times, as in Classical Greek pieces, bodies, top sections, rims were thrown separately, hardened somewhat and then added and turned together to give very large symmetrically silhouetted store jars with smooth surfaces to take the intricate painting of gods and heroes (*406*).

Generally, there are three main ways of section throwing:

1 Throw all the pieces, let them stiffen and, like the Greeks, join and turn them together – for me the least effective and most lifeless way.

2 Join two (or more) forms together when they are still soft enough to allow throwing to continue. For example one bowl shape inverted onto another. The thickness of the 'base' of the top bowl is made into the neck of what has now become a large bottle with unbroken line from base to neck (196-200); many large cider jars are made like this (*201*).

192 Smack and thump a large lump into the middle with the wheel gently turning, hands dry.

193 Open with two hands, move down and then out – test the thickness of the base with a pin.

194 Lift the rudimentary cylinder with a collaring action.

195 After collaring, knuckle and thumb held wide make a good grip for a large lump; the inside fingers are bunched together and slightly cupped.

3 Add a coil of clay to a form that has been allowed to dry sufficiently to withstand the pressure and weight of new clay. This way for me is the most satisfactory and can be used either to follow the line of the original throwing or to articulate the form so that the added coil heralds a change of direction that accentuates the join. The added coil can be rolled out of soft clay and wrapped round the top of the stiffened form which has been roughened up and slurried to receive it; the coil is then thrown (any irregularities cut off with a pin) and allowed to stiffen ready for another coil . . . and another. To speed this process considerably I *throw* the 'coil', and in this way can bring much more clay at one time on to the waiting rim. Furthermore, as it is thrown the coil is perfectly centred. It is remarkable how stiff the original throwing can be allowed to get before the very soft and sometimes quite large thrown 'coils' are added (202-206, *colour 12*). Once joined and the throwing completed then the drying process must be slowed to allow the two parts to even out (i.e. don't put it in a warm place). This 'thrown coil' principle can be extended for very wide-rimmed vessels by throwing the large wide soft 'coil' on a bat, inverting the bat and clay onto the waiting pot and only cutting the bat away when the 'coil' is both located in position and the fingers have pressed home the soft clay. Throwing then continues with the very soft clay riding on top of the original form and giving no trouble in centring (207-210).

196 Score well and slurry liberally the drier bottom section of the form centred on the wheel.

197 Place a loose bat onto the rim of the damp, thrown top section, to turn it over.

198 Hold the bat, to which the top section is still stuck, and guide the two forms together. Smooth over the join.

199 Wire off the top bat and continue joining inside and outside by throwing the two rims together.

200 The wet 'base' of the top bowl is now the top of the joined form. Throw it to become the rim or neck – or add more!

201 Stoneware cider jar by Ray Finch.

202 Measure the outside of the scored and slurried rim with callipers.

203 Throw a soft collar of clay, measure, wire through and lift it off.

204 Offer it up to the waiting stiffer base form.

205 Join the two pieces together.

206 Throw the soft top.

207 Keep the soft wide thrown collar on the bat.

208 Join it on well before wiring it off the bat.

209 Keep the clay moist by feeding water from a squeezed sponge on to the other hand with the wheel turning.

210 Continue throwing the soft wet collar.

211 Place on a thrown ring of soft clay to make a goblet or pedestal pot.

212 Join it on and throw it up – pot held centred by pads of clay.

213 Add a foot to a dish or plate by placing a very soft coil on to the scored and slurried base. Mitre the join and finger the coil well down.

214 Throw the coil on and then up.

215 Pin off the excess clay.

216 Using a taut wire you can cut 'legs' out of the soft clay foot. Make sure they are robust enough to hold the plate without warping during the firing.

An exciting new range of forms and pots of great size await the thrower bold enough (and with a kiln large enough!) to tackle these methods (*430*). Not only necks, rims and whole new sections can be added like this but at the other end of the pot, feet and pedestals can be added in a similar way (211-216, *2*).

The danger is that the concept of the whole pot will be lost in this multiplicity of processes. But there is danger in every additional process whether in making, decorating or firing. A sensitive awareness of form, colour and texture is essential at all times. It is what makes in the end for a good potter. We can all aspire to this sensitivity towards materials, processes and forms: nothing ventured . . . . .

Rims and galleries

The function of some pots demands a more robust and thickened edge, the wooden kitchen spoon banged against a thin edge will soon chip it. Again, some clays will only stay in shape if the rim is thickened. Like most things in pottery there is more than one way of achieving this. The wall of the pot can be thrown up and from very early on in the throwing process a thickened rim allowed to ride up on top of it. Pressure with the thumb and fingers of one hand on the side of the wall just below the top, together with a slight pressure downwards on the rim with the fingers of the other hand will almost immediately produce a thickened rim as the wheel spins freely round (217). Or a chamois leather can be wrapped round the edge of the wall and a squeezing pressure applied, again just below the top. This will give a very smooth, well-rounded rim (218). Another rather different approach is to 'bend' the top half an inch or so of the rim (1·3 cm) – depending on the size of the vessel – right over outwards or inwards to give an edge of double thickness. There is a danger of trapping air as the edge folds round but with many open clays this doesn't matter because the clay can 'breathe' enough anyway, and if the clay wall is allowed to fall over slowly and evenly the air will be expelled before the pressure of the fingers seals the clay over (219, 220). Many potters use this method, and only slightly modify it, to form a gallery or shelf on which a lid may sit. It has the virtue of giving a very positive seating for the lid as well as a robust edge and is achieved by pushing the *inward* bending rim, as it slowly falls over, diagonally back towards the wall of the pot (221-223). The other main way of making a gallery is to split the thickened rim in half with finger or rib, sending one half of the clay inwards to form the horizontal ledge for the lid whilst the other half moves up or slightly out to form a retaining wall (224, 225). Both ways can be effective and must be used to fit in with the overall feeling or style of the pot. On either kind a firm shelf for the lid can be achieved by pressing a rib or finger into the channel to make an angle, rather than a vague taper into which the lid might slip and wedge tight as it fires, this can give endless trouble when the pot finally emerges from the kiln.

217 Form a sturdy rim with the pressure of one finger on top, and a squeeze between thumb and finger just below.

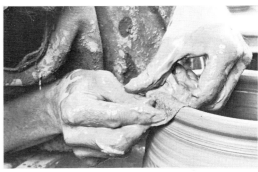

218 Use a chamois leather to thicken a rim.

219 A thick rim is often made by turning over the clay at the top. You can form a 'double' thickness in this way.

220 Ease the clay over gently so the air is expelled as the clay bends over.

221 Or thin out the clay before bending it inwards.

222 Keep control of the bending rim with the fingers of the left hand.

223 Let the clay go over slowly, push diagonally inwards with the index finger of the left hand. You can get a sturdy outer rim with this method.

224 Split a thickened rim with a finger

225 Then sharpen up the angle with a rib.

Lids

The lids themselves are thrown, or thrown and turned, in a variety of ways usually determined by how they fit onto the pot (226). The illustrations show the main types (227). Measuring lids can be a frustrating business; many potters will confirm my findings that clays have 'memory' that makes lids dry and fire in peculiar ways that result in poor lid fitting: if you tend to throw a lid out flat, and then bend up the edge to achieve the measurement you want, you may well find that in some clays the lid flattens out again as it dries and fires; conversely if you tend to make a rather bowl-like lid and flatten it out to the required width then the lid will tend to curl up again. All this makes lid fitting difficult and means that you must know your clay and your throwing habits. Observe what happens, then one way of coping is to compensate in advance for its behaviour, the results will at least be consistent (228-238).

Knobs on lids are best applied by 'skimming', that is, minimal turning the lid when leather-hard, and scoring and slurrying a central area, then firmly pressing on a lump of soft clay which can be thrown with the minimum of water into any knob shape desired (239). This is preferable to leaving a large amount of clay under the lid to be turned away later, because this almost always results in a wooden finish to the lid and knob.

Lips and spouts

Pouring vessels such as tea-pots, coffee-jugs and batter-bowls present a special challenge to the thrower. They have to work, that is they have to pour, and if possible not drip. A lip can be 'pulled' from the wall of the pot by the gentle pressure of one wetted finger, whilst the wall on either side of this point is held by the thumb and finger of the other hand. The actual rim's edge is very important for this operation and potters get up to all sorts of tricks to achieve a good-looking lip that will also pour well. One way is to pinch up a crescent of clay from the rim of the pot before pulling the actual lip over. This gives a nice rising lip with a sharp edge that will cut off the liquid, but if it is too sharp it will chip too easily (240-242). Another way is to leave a sharp edge on the inside of the rim and then pull over the lip, so that this sharp edge becomes the cutting edge for the liquid. Some potters give jugs a throat to channel the liquid out (243-244), others even add lips of flattened pieces of clay which they model onto the jug, or even cut spout-like forms in half and add these as a kind of half-lip half-spout solution to the problem. There is no one way, and pouring vessels are a constant source of personal expression for the thrower (*369-373, back cover 1*).

Spouts are usually thrown on a hump of clay, some potters using a straight stick inside, instead of a finger, to enable them to pull up the long straight – or slightly tapering – neck (245-248). Some potters, such as

226 Throwing a lid on a hump of clay; the top of the clay is re-centred each time and a new lid is thrown; spouts can also be thrown like this.

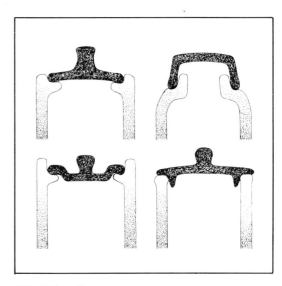

227 Lid sections.

228 Open a groove in the centred lump.

229 Form the knob by pressing in with a fast wheel.

230 Make a vertical wall which you can measure for fitting.

231 Bend the horizontal edge over.

232 Wire through, grasp the knob and lift as the knife releases the lid from the bat.

233 The knob can be left as a ring or hollowed to allow air through.

234 Throw a wide cylinder with no base and gather in the top.

235 Use a fast wheel to gather the top in further.

236 Throw the overhanging rim, the flange must be turned at a later stage.

237 Throw a short bowl-shape and split the rim with the two index fingers.

238 True up the flange with a rib.

239 Add a soft ring of clay to form a ring-knob or use a lump of clay for a solid knob.

David Leach, cut the spout off the wheel and let it dry to leather hardness before trimming it and fitting it to the pot (*370*); or, as I do, you can cut it straight off the wheel and put it on the leather-hard pot, making a virtue of the fact that the clay is soft and can very easily be smoothed into the harder clay of the tea- or coffee-pot body. I like a fast wheel, and I like to use the rib to remove the slurry from the spout so that I can pick it up easily, but here again opinions differ (249). All agree, however, that some clays will go on twisting as they dry and fire, making spout fitting a tricky business. When you know your clay you can allow for this continuing movement: when you cut the end of the spout – if you choose to do this (and in general the cut-ended spout does seem to pour better) – cut it slightly crooked as in the illustration (250-253).

240 Pinch up a crescent of clay from the thickened rim.

241 Slide two fingers from side to side to compress the rim of the lip.

242 To pull the lip, hold the sides of the lip with finger and thumb and stroke over with the other hand.

243 Give the jug a throat to channel the liquid.

244 Make sure the lip is straight.

245 Open out a wide-based cylinder and gather it in.

246 Use finger, knuckle, thumb on each hand with a fast speed to collar in the spout.

247 A stick helps to make the spout taller and opening smaller.

248 Rib off the slurry so that you can pick up the spout.

249 Wire the spout through diagonally.

250 Offer up the spout to the pot to check where it should go; the wet end will mark where the holes should go.

251 Use a hole cutter or drill bit to make a pattern of holes.

Handles and lugs

Handles and lugs are usually added to a pot when it is nearing a leather-hard state. There are numerous very different ways of making handles, including cutting them out of a lump of clay with looped wire formers, rolling, slabbing or press-moulding them, and throwing them, i.e. either the complete handle, or cutting up a thrown cylinder into strips; but the most universal way seems to be to 'pull' the handle from a lump of well-wedged clay. One way of pulling is to hold up a firmly-wedged lump of clay with one hand while the other well-wetted hand pulls and strokes the clay down into a long, only slightly tapering section. From this long tail several smaller pieces can be detached to form handles that need only a little more pulling to complete them. Or again, many short stubs can be pulled and laid by on a board (254).

Before you add the handles, score thoroughly and wet the pot at the point of join; then you pick up a stub, mould it to the pot, and then the completed handle is pulled out of this stub to be joined lower down the pot at the appropriate place (255-256). How the handle is pulled, what section is arrived at, flat or rounded, ridged or smooth, and how the handle is attached at both ends, are all aspects that leave considerable room for individual interpretation and expression (*191, 420, 328, colour 12*). My own way for example is to push a rolled-out piece of firm clay onto the scored and slurried top of the pot, weld it firmly home with much finger- and thumb-pressure, then hold the pot horizontal, allowing the handle to point downwards, so that only a few pulls with a wet hand will complete the handle and allow me to attach it firmly at the other end with whatever 'finish' I feel the pot merits (257-261). On larger pots I leave the pot upright on the bat on which it was thrown – and – never letting go –

252 Press the spout home, smooth it in all the way round or leave a line showing where it was joined.

253 You can add lugs for a cane handle or make a side clay handle. Cut the spout slightly crooked with wire or knife; it will go on twisting and straighten up in the firing.

254 Pull the lump down into a tail with a wet hand and cut off a stump with the table's edge.

255 Score the leather hard jug with a knife.

256 Push on the slurried or wetted half-pulled stump, continue pulling and join at the base as in 260.

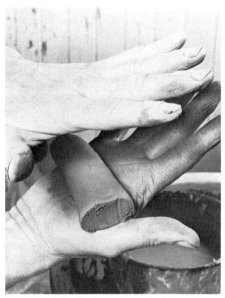

257 Pat and roll a lump into a handle stub.

258 Push it onto the scored and slurried jug.

259 Hold the jug horizontal and use a wet hand to stroke the handle down.

260 Support the wall on the inside while you push the end of the handle onto the jug – no scoring is needed if the clay is soft enough.

261 You can give differently shaped jugs different handle sections and finishes at top and bottom.

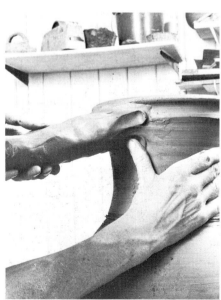

262 Thumb on a very large lump for a big jug – you must score and slurry the join before you push the clay on firmly.

263 Use two wet hands to pull and stroke the clay out to make the handle.

264 Press the end on firmly and use a roll of clay to fill in the gap between body and handle.

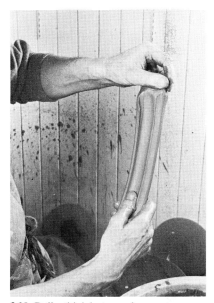

265 Pull a thick but even lug.

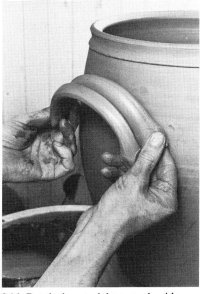

266 Put the lug straight on to the side of the leather-hard pot.

267 Smooth in one edge and shape the lug to a suitable curve.

pull the handle with both hands with the sort of movements one might use to pull in a rope from the side of a ship (262-264). Very wide handles with quite interesting sections can be made in this way. Once again it must be the potter's sensitivity to form that tells him how far he can go – you are aiming at a pot that is a whole and has a unity through all its parts.

Not all thrown pots are round

Most people think of the wheel as producing only round pots, but it has been a traditional practice for many hundreds of years to make oval and even squared shapes from round wheel-made forms. If the clay is caught at the right state, before rims have hardened and bases stiffened too much, bowls, dishes and even lidded pots can be eased or beaten into non-round shapes (402). The traditional oval pie dish is made by cutting a lozenge or thin leaf shape from the base of the dish. Cut the base through underneath with the wire, push the walls near the base together, to close up the gap. Some potters put back the soft cut-out piece on top of the join and firmly press the clay base flat again; this probably does reinforce the join (272-275). I have often made squared dishes and lidded boxes simply by squaring the tops as soon as I have thrown the pot, and then (remembering *not* to wire through the base) beating the sides as soon as the clay stiffened (276-282, *270*). As long as the base is not left too long it can always be cut through later, and the fact that it is stuck fast to the bat means that the base does not distort while the pot is being shaped. An extension of this principle is used today by potters who want even squarer or more irregular shapes. They cut the pot away from the base entirely, leaving themselves with what is virtually a sleeve of clay which is relatively easy to bend into all kinds of shapes, and when suitably stiff, add it back onto a thrown or pressed-out base of even thickness. Some squared dishes by Ray Finch, and the more amorphous pots and boxes of Joanna Constantinidis are made in this way (283).

Once we accept that the wheel need not be restrictive, making only certain shapes, then new forms become possible, and the wheel can be used to produce parts of forms that are added together at the right stage. Hans Coper has produced a range of unique forms made in this way over the last 30 years generally using a narrow range of clays and firing in electric kilns (430). These pots distil the essence of his feelings for certain forms and textures. Pots made in this way still retain their thrown quality, as can be seen in the porcelain pots made by Sheila Casson where

268 Give the ends a finish and go over the curve again.

269 A lug used on top of a lid to make a strap handle.

cutaway sections have been complemented and balanced by cut-out and added pieces (271). The wheel is a willing and versatile tool; some people are more flamboyant in their expression, others are more restrained . . . and, whichever you are, as with all processes, you must use your own sensitivity and discrimination to make a good pot.

270 Stoneware lidded pot, squared after throwing, by Michael Casson.

271 Piercing used as decoration in thrown porcelain forms by Sheila Casson.

272 Put the wired-off pot onto a sanded bat; cut a 'leaf' shape right through the base and lift out.

273 Squeeze the opening together from the base, the rim will go oval naturally.

274 Place the 'leaf' shape back and press and smooth it on top of the closed seam.

275 Scrape the base flat with rib or metal kidney.

276 Use the fingers to square off the rim as soon as it is thrown. You can beat the sides more square later.

277 Accentuate the squaring with finger lines.

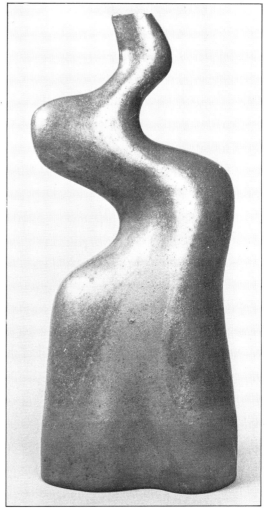

283 Tall form made from thrown shape, reduced stoneware by Joanna Constantinidis.

278 Measure carefully for the lid before squaring.

279 The inside finger, and outside finger and thumb do the squaring from the bottom to the top of the form.

280 Make sure the rim is quite square while the pot is wet, you can beat the sides when leathery but the top easily cracks when drier.

281 Measure under the lid before squaring.

282 Move the fingers firmly outwards, the lid must be put onto the pot as soon as possible and gently beaten into the squared shape, moving it round so that it fits in every position.

Decorating

When we make a mark in clay we are decorating. There is no aspect of pottery that gives as much chance for individual expression and imagination as decoration. It is impossible to say when it begins, so that some potters do not even think of themselves as decorators. For example, when a handbuilder starts to make a form, the decoration may begin at the same time, as when the pinching movement gives rhythmic indentations to the surface of a thumb-pot, or when a coiler smoothes some coils but allows others to remain, to give a texture to the surface. Decoration only ends when the pot is out of the last fire – and even then there are some potters, in Africa and the South Sea Islands, who rub vegetable juices into the pot as it emerges red-hot from the fire. The juices make the pot less porous but also stain in a decorative way the patterns scored in the clay. And who is to say that even time does not play its part in giving a pot its final decoration? The irridescence on a Persian bowl long buried in sand, the crackle on a Sung pot enhanced by the stains of age, both add to the decoration (*399*). Some potters would admire these fortuitous effects, chance plays its game in all pottery they would say,

284 Group of jugs with painted decoration by Alison Britton.

others might hope for more control. The one principle of decoration that all potters seem to agree on is that decoration should enhance the form, otherwise don't decorate.

The choice then is, when and how to decorate. What kind of marks you make, or what 'subject' you use, abstract or representational, is entirely up to you. One potter may decide that a drawing of the Tower of London on the side of a pot is just what is needed, another finds that a series of lines, dots and areas satisfies his feeling for enhancing form (284). Lucie Rie for example, has used thin, spare lines and inlaid circles to wonderful effect on her beautifully quiet pots (293). What all potters will have to face each time they decorate is the fact that they are using the processes and materials of pottery: sooner or later expression will be limited by what these will allow the decorator to do. It may help to look back at the extraordinarily varied examples from history to find some balance between the 'how' and 'what' of decoration. The very first pots we know of are decorated with simple chevron patterns that imitate basket weaving, (probably basket-ware preceded pottery (285)). Later, the geometric patterns gave way to abstract animals and plants; it seems that the potters could not contain their innate desire to decorate the clay in some way.

285 Handbuilt earthenware Saxon food vessel with incised 'chevron' decoration.

When to decorate

Generally speaking there are certain times when it is most effective to decorate in particular ways:

1 Before biscuit firing

When the clay is from soft to leather- or cheese-hard:

Cutting, fluting, beating to alter the shape. Incising, inlay (to be completed when much drier). Adding soft clay – 'sprigging' adding harder clay shapes. Piercing. Impressing. Using slip – dip, pour, paint, trail, wax-resist, paper-resist.

When the clay is from leather-hard to dry:

Painting with pigments, i.e. metal oxides with water, possibly a little clay and/or gum added. Rubbing in oxides.

2 After biscuit firing

Before glazing, i.e. under glaze:

Painting with pigments, i.e. metal oxides or bought under-glaze colours, with water and probably a little gum. Rubbing in oxides.

After glazing, i.e. on top of the unfired glaze (over tin glaze, this is called maiolica, faience, or Delft):

Painting with pigments, i.e. metal oxides or bought colours with water and possibly a little gum and glaze. Wax-resist – poured or brushed on before painting with pigments and/or applying a second glaze.

3 After glaze firing

On top of the fired glaze (NB a second glaze firing at a lower temperature is necessary):

Painting with metals to obtain lustres including gold and silver. On-glaze, 'enamel' painting usually with bought prepared colours.

No list of methods will ever be definitive, someone will always come along and innovate. Here are some examples of the more usual decoration techniques. Although they are treated separately, remember that they can very often be combined.

Incising

This really covers any method that takes clay *away* from the form being made, and includes cutting, carving, fluting, anything that makes a cut mark in the surface (*289, 301, 370, 372, 425, colour 7*). It is done usually when the clay is from very soft to cheese-hard. If very soft, the strokes

286 Bamboo fluting tool.

287 Incised marks – each tool gives a characteristic mark.

will have to be swift and deft if the form is not to distort; at leather-hardness more time can be taken. Tools include implements of bamboo (286); carved, notched, toothed wooden tools; metal; bone; slate; even porcupine quills have been used! A looped wire turning-tool gives a deep, controllable line (287). Even whole areas can be carved away at the firmer, leather-hard stage (*291*).

In handbuilding, where the clay is usually initially stiffer than in throwing, the applications of incising as a decorative method are legion; pinched or coiled pots are easily textured with lines and dots as in the very earliest pottery, or line-and-area drawings, perhaps of birds, plants, etc., can be made in the cheese-hard clay. Press-moulded forms and slab constructions are by their very nature firm and easier to handle, so that incising techniques can be precisely controlled, either laid out and cut before the panels are joined into the slab box or before the clay is taken from the mould (*292*). Eileen Nisbet inscribes her swirling lines by moving the tool and dish in a kind of dance to produce the decoration on her dish (*290*).

What is not so often realised is that thrown forms also lend themselves to incising; if the walls are the right thickness, even whole areas can be sliced away with a taut wire just after the pot has been thrown (294, 299). It is possible to carry out these techniques even before the throwing is completed to get a unique kind of decorative effect. The incising – cutting of lines, nicks, even small sliced-off areas – is made in the rather thicker

288 Carved decoration in cast bone-china form by Jacqueline Poncelet.

289 Small porcelain bowl with incised, carved, pierced and added clay decoration by Victor Margrie.

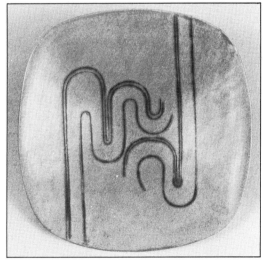

290 Earthenware press-moulded dish with incised decoration stained with oxide under a honey glaze, by Eileen Nisbet.

291 Stoneware bowl, thrown with cut sides by Bernard Leach.

292 Handbuilt tiles with scratched and painted decoration by Alison Britton.

293 Oxidised porcellanous pot with inlaid lines and circles by Lucie Rie.

walls of the half-thrown pot, then the inside hand of the thrower carries on throwing and swells the form upwards and outwards, changing the incisions in a dramatic way (295-297). Gently ribbing the surface as this is happening makes a further decorative permutation possible.

Try out your ideas, this sort of creative playing on the wheel, or with handbuilt forms before they have become too stiff, can lead to some of the most delightful and spontaneous results, because the forms are freshly made and the clay still pliant. Look at the work of Richard Batterham who cuts facets and strong lines in his work as he makes it (298), or the work of Terry Bell-Hughes who incises his teapots to give an almost fruit-like appearance (372); these are just two of the many potters who like to decorate the clay at the earliest moment on the wheel. Incising in unfired clay is a fundamental technique of prime importance because inlay, piercing and many of the uses of slip depend upon it, and it can be used in conjunction with impressing and stamping, adding clay and even painting.

294 You can cut slices off a thickly thrown form immediately after you have thrown it, or wait for it to stiffen slightly.

295 Throw a thick cylinder and experiment with incised marks.

296 With one hand continue throwing outwards.

297 Steady the top and swell the form out again with one hand.

Impressing

Clay is not removed in the impressing technique, it is simply pressed into the form. Some of the very earliest pots found in Britain have impressed rows of diagonal lines that were made in all probability with the potter's fingernails. Anything in fact that can make a mark will serve either singly or repeated to build up a pattern. You can use all kinds of things – the list has as many entries as people find objects – from buttons to string, from seeds to the heavily-veined leaves of some plants (300). You can also make your own impressing 'tools' by carving them in the end grain of wood, or into any close-grained wood, cutting plaster of Paris or making a cast of plaster of Paris from a clay master. Probably the easiest is by incising and carving clay stamps which are then fired to biscuit temperature. Potters usually use this method to make the name-seals that identify their work. You can make patterns all the way round a cylindrical shape made of any of the above materials to form a drum-like stamp, called a roulette, which when rolled across or round a form will leave the impressions stamped in a continuous band in the clay; if mounted on stiff wire axles and provided with a handle they are very easy to use. Ladi Kwali uses a roulette which she rolls round with her fingers to decorate the edges of her monumental pots (427). In 18th century Staffordshire, brass roulettes with extremely intricate patterns were used to great effect, the glaze covering but not obscuring the tiny details. Short lengths of string, rope or braided cord will give a softer result.

Impressed decoration is really a question of selecting your 'mark maker' and choosing the right moment in the making of the form to impress your

298 Incised stoneware dish by Richard Batterham.

299 Taut wire on small metal harp.

57

decoration. This will differ greatly according to the type of forming process concerned. For example, to wrap grass or string round a pinch pot, or to use a piece of coarse-grained cloth on a thrown pot, will mean that the clay in both cases will have to be soft. Moreover, you will have to support the form from the inside while the impressing is carried out; you will have to do this with practically all impressions made on wheel-made work, the exception being in the use of some roulettes which will cut into drier thrown forms quite easily. On the other hand, if you are going to roll out or stamp a pattern on a sheet of clay prepared for a slab pot, or gently but firmly beat a coiled pot with a textured wooden beater, the clay can be considerably harder, and therefore can probably allow more precise placing of the pattern and more intricate layout of pattern or texture on the forms. As in all decoration, this can be a mixed blessing, the more options you have or the more easily you can decorate the more you tend to overdo it; the type of impressions that have to be made in a split second – or at least those that stop you from going on too long – often turn out the best. But experience should also lead to restraint, even with the most elaborate techniques. Handbuilders, especially those using slab or press-moulding techniques really have nothing to stop them. I have known all manner of things to be rolled into such surfaces prior to making, seeds and sawdust for example which burn away during firing. But throwers too should take heart from the simple, strong decoration that Hamada has used on some of his bowls, achieved by impressing and incising in a zig-zag pattern round the outside horizontal wall (*302*). Nearly all the impressions, made by whatever method, tend to show the marks made in a shallow relief of even and consistent depth so that they lend themselves to staining with thin solutions of metal oxides and water or slip, (see p.68). And finally the glaze itself will run and possibly pool into the impressed decorations to add to the surface interest, point up changes of form and enhance the overall effect of the work.

300 Impressed marks: experiment with different objects.

Roulettes made of wood or cast in plaster of Paris from clay originals.

Inlay

Marks in clay, whether incised or impressed, can also be filled up with different coloured slips or clays until eventually they are made flush with the original surface of the work, to form a coloured inlay decoration (*303*). This inlaying technique is best started when the clay form is still reasonably damp so that the inlaid material will adhere more readily. In addition the coloured slips or clays used must be compatible with the clay of the pot. A good way to ensure this is either to stain the actual body being used with metal oxides (see section on *Slip)* or to incorporate at least some of this body as part of the inlaid clays. There are exceptions to this, for example I have always found that a mixture of 50% ball clay and 50% China clay, stained or not, will adhere in or on most stoneware clays fired to quite high temperatures (1300°C+). This is most useful because the colour contrast with most iron-bearing stoneware clays can be used to great advantage.

The indentations should be generously filled in, that is, considerably above the level of the surface, because whether you use thick slip or soft plastic clay as your inlay, both of these will shrink more than the clay form itself (which has already undergone considerable shrinkage to get to the soft to leather-hard state). In fact if you use thick slip – and I find this easiest for inlaying fine lines, using a brush – you will have to go over the areas again to 'top up' the level of the inlay. Rub in the clay, or brush on the slip, you don't need to be too accurate. Once the inlay has dried to stiff leather-hardness you can begin to scrape down the surface with a blade – old hack saw, 'backed' razor blade, knife or metal kidney, to leave the inlay only in the incised or impressed design. It is wise to test an area first, because it's very easy, in one's impatience to see the pattern again, to start to 'clean off' too soon, and drag the inlaid clays out of their

301 Northern Celadon pot with incised decoration, Sung dynasty China 12th century AD.

302 Bowl with incised and impressed pattern by Hamada.

304 Incise, then fill in with slip.

305 Or you can use soft plastic clay to fill in with.

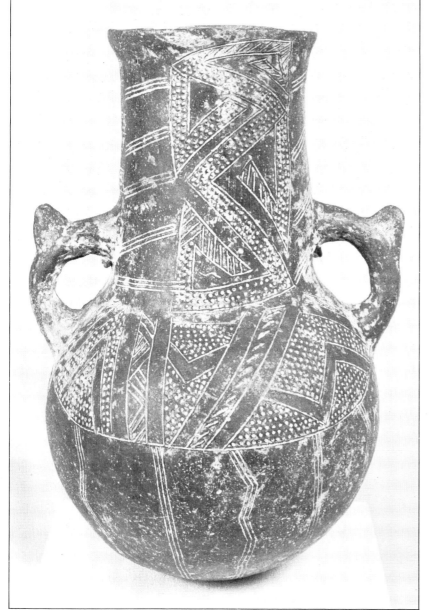

303 Handbuilt coiled pot with white clay inlay, Cyprus about 2,000 BC.

306 When dry or nearly so, scrape away the excess slip.

grooves, or to start removing too much from a wider area of inlay and so produce rather unsightly 'dips' in the surface of the form. I believe in waiting until the clays are practically dry. By then you have almost forgotten what the pattern was so that the scraping away becomes a real discovery again (304-306). The inlay wares later called Mishima from Korea of the 13th century onwards are among the finest examples from history of this technique (*colour 9*). Today many potters use it, and when decorating my own landscape pots I frequently use an inlay of semi-porcelain clay into a deep-red-firing fireclay body. You can also inlay glaze, but remember that this technique begins with good clean lines (areas of glaze do not inlay so well) incised or impressed at the soft- to leather-hard stage.

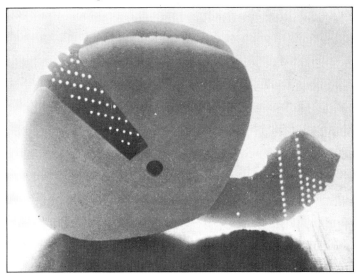

307 Porcelain sculptured form with pierced decoration by Eileen Nisbet.

308 Bowl with pierced decoration, 13th century Persia.

Piercing

If incising and impressing are carried on and on they eventually go right through the wall of the pot. Pierced decoration can be extremely effective in visually uniting the inside and outside surfaces of forms, whether thrown or handbuilt, and a whole battery of piercing tools can be useful including thin bladed knives, drill bits of all sizes, needles and hollow metal tubes, (squared and shaped hollow cutters were used by 18th century Leeds potters). Piercing through clay can begin when it is very soft indeed. Walter Keeler has used this method: when he has finished throwing a pot, he makes holes in it in or near the rim, by rubbing the clay wall through with the pressure of wet thumb and finger to give a 'torn' look to the perforations made. They fit the free, almost casual thrown form exactly and give a lively decoration to the top half of the throwing. Usually, however, it is easier to leave cutting right through the clay until it is soft to leathery in hardness: that is, it should be soft enough to pierce and cut out lines, and therefore shapes, without distorting the form in the process. If the clay is harder than this, *drilling* may be possible, but *cutting* will almost certainly result in cracking and ruining the pot. Burrs thrown up by blade or drill-bit can cause a problem: you run the risk that if you try to clean them off by sponging and cleaning, the surface and even the form becomes flabby. If you leave the burrs you will end up with sharp, visually unpleasant and even dangerous edges. So do some of the cleaning when the pot is dry, using a knife or a slightly damp sponge. You can do some more after the biscuit firing (if you are not firing to a very high temperature).

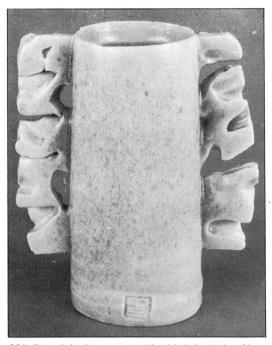

309 Porcelain thrown pot with added clay 'wings' by Colin Pearson.

Eileen Nisbet makes sculptured forms that use the play of light through drill screens and grilles in porcelain bodies; each hole is drilled and counter sunk to give the sharpest possible image (*307*). Historically pierced and

310 Stoneware pot with fluted rim and added clay decoration by Walter Keeler.

cut patterns have been used by many potters: the Chinese still set rice seeds, the thickness of the porcelain clay wall, into the pot so that they fire away leaving a pierced shape over which the glaze runs to give a window of clear glaze (*308*). This technique needs great control but by knowing the behaviour of a glaze it is quite possible for today's potter to cut patterns of small thin holes and shapes over which the glaze will run to form such traceries.

Adding clay

The method of adding clay to a pot or form is best carried out at one of two times: either when the clay form is soft, in which case soft clay can be joined to it simply by pushing it on and smoothing, beating or pressing it home; or when the form is drier, by keying the surface (i.e. roughening it) applying slip or slurry and adding similarly stiffer clay shapes to this area (*311*). This latter method is called 'sprigging'. No doubt the inventive potter will discover many states in between when some decorative effect can be captured, but to begin with I feel these two stages are best.

While there may be many more ways of applying clay to handbuilt pots than to thrown pots (see p. 24), the method is certainly not exclusive to handbuilding, as many fine historical and contemporary examples of thrown pots can testify. Medieval British jugs, sometimes considered the finest pots made in these islands, were often embellished with pads and rolls of soft clay – added, it seems, just after the potter's wheel had stopped turning. Some later medieval jugs, where the decoration has been added at a later stage, even have modelled knights on horseback galloping round the strong shoulders. A contemporary potter, Walter Keeler, uses soft pads of clay smoothed into the lower part of the thrown wall to echo the pot's convoluted rim (*310*). When thrown forms have

311 Adding clay shapes. Use soft clay, then no scoring is needed.

become leather-hard, then coils, rolls, pads, in fact any shape at all (provided the thickness is not so excessive that it might cause distortion to the wall it adheres to) can be added by pressing and gently beating them on. Keying will only be necessary if the clay has become stiffer or more specifically if beating or other ways of integrating clay and additions are ruled out for some reason (309). For example long soft snakes of clay can be wrapped round thrown pots when still softish but firm and integrated with the pot, either by a series of little finger pressures that show as tiny decorative nicks in the clay or by being smoothed on with a damp sponge (312, 313).

Or added clay can take the form of a delicately modelled piece of clay, either made as a single piece, or taken from a mould from which many repeats might come: this can hardly be fingered, beaten or luted with sponge and water; it must be keyed and slipped. The slurry used to key the sprigs on is gently eased away if it should squeeze out from underneath. This method is an example of the sprig as it was used in the 18th century especially by the Staffordshire potters such as Josiah Wedgwood (314) or by the German salt glaze potters of the 17th century.

314 Making a sprig at the Wedgwood factory.

315 Place on rolls, balls, etc., of a different coloured clay; the softer it is the more it will spread.

316 Roll it in; you can put other colours on this first pressing and roll again.

312 Large pot, thrown and coiled, with added clay and painted decoration, Persia, 1500 BC.

317 Press down with your thumb then roll in harder shapes arranged as you want them. Use the same clay as the base tile or differently coloured clays for contrast.

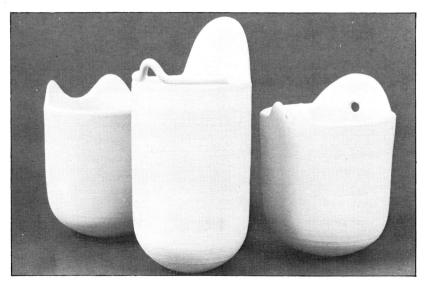

313 Porcelain forms by Sheila Casson, thrown bowls with added thrown pieces.

1 Press-moulded dish with brush decoration by Hamada.

2 Chün dish with copper splashes from Sung China 960-1279.

3 Italian Maiolica drug jar, Faenza 1480.

4 Lustre plate from Deruta, Italy, early 16th century.

5 Pedestal dish by Paul Philp; agate-ware under a transparent glaze.

6 13th century painted Persian pot with modelled bird head, copper glaze.

7 Bernard Leach, stoneware pot with incised bird under a tenmoku glaze.

8 Painted stoneware plate by Eric Mellon.

9 Lidded box, Korean, Koryo dynasty, inlaid decoration, 12th century.

10 Stoneware pot with reduced copper painting from Korea, Yi dynasty circa 17th century.

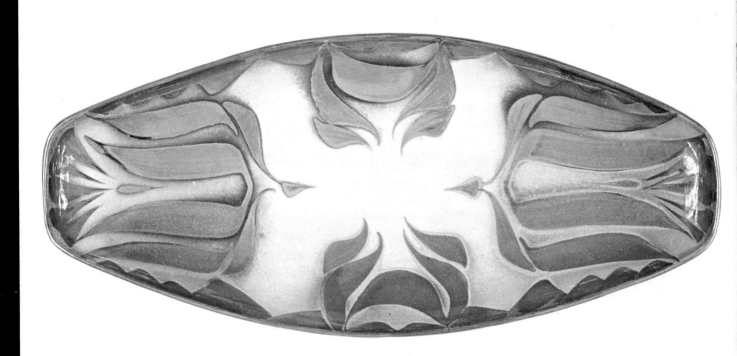

11 Lustre-painted press-moulded dish by Alan Caiger-Smith.

13 Lustre-painted hand basin, Hispano-Moresque, 15th century.

12 Large stoneware jug with wiped slip decoration under a tenmoku glaze by Michael Casson.

14 Persian Minai bowl with Islamic script round the outside and with overglaze decoration and gilding, 13th century.

15 Coiled stoneware pot with painted decoration by Elizabeth Fritsch.

16 Covered pot with multicoloured oxide splashes under a lead glaze, T'ang China, 618-906 AD.

18 Lead-glazed Raku bucket pot by Walter Keeler.

17 Tall bottle thrown by Lucie Rie, with matt oxidised stoneware glaze.

19 Glazed tiles by Lynne Reeve showing degrees of opacity.

20 Pre-dynastic Egyptian jar, before 3000 BC, low-fired earthenware.

21 Glazed tiles by Lynne Reeve showing (a) copper–oxidised, reduced; (b) cobalt–oxidised, reduced; (c) iron–oxidised, reduced.
(The colours shown are approximate)

Clays of different colours were used sometimes on a layer of slip of contrasting colour. Even quite curved sprigs and large medallions of clay with crests and seals were added in this way (419). Sometimes a softer clay pad was added to the surface and the 'seal' was then stamped in this.

In many senses the handbuilder is often adding clay most of the time while the form is being built up, but more specifically the surfaces of handbuilt forms lend themselves particularly well to adding clay – especially at the softer, more pliable and spontaneous stage. All the main handbuilding methods are suitable.

Moreover, apart from merely adding clay you may also add clay of a different colour and texture so that the surface is greatly enriched in a visual and tactile sense. You can change the texture of the clay body, by adding different types of clays together – a coarser fireclay for example will have a marked effect on the surface, or by adding grogs and sands of various mesh size and differing qualities. Some sands carry iron particles and nodules that burn and blister the surface of a clay form to give it the appearance of a volcanic eruption. Add sawdust or coaldust to this and

318 Large handbuilt Jomon pot, with coiled, incised and added clay decoration, Japan 500 BC.

you may even emulate the craters of the moon. As always, experiments and notes taken of observations are essential.

Pinching I feel lends itself to adding clays in smaller amounts, rolls and pads smoothed in as the fingers move round and round, but coilers can be more dramatic as they build and beat, adding snakes and even whole areas of soft clay (*428*); Jomon pots from early Japan will be an inspiration here (*318*). The main problem remains: how to integrate all these separate elements: forming methods; decoration processes; glazing and firing? In adding clay to coiled pots the problem is for once perhaps minimised because coils, pads and rolls of clay can be built in and on as the making proceeds: colour and texture altered and controlled as the form gets larger. In slabbed boxes each wall of the pot can be planned out and clay added before the final shapes are cut.

It is well to remember here two interesting types of adding: *rolled inlay*, and the use of *harder clay shapes*. (Rolled inlay can be used for tiles and press-moulding as well, but it is as well to describe it here because it is easier to plan slab pots than any other kind.) If very soft, thin rolls, blobs and shapes of clays of different colour from the form itself (perhaps white clay and red clay on a light tan stoneware clay for example, or stained white clays can work as well) are placed in position on a slab or sheet of clay and gently rolled in, they spread and distort to give a decorative effect (315, 316). To a certain extent the distortions are unpredictable, but with more experience more control is possible. So long as the sheet of clay is not too hard and the added clay very soft the rolling pin will do the work and more clay can be added and rolled on to build up as much complexity as you wish.

The use of harder clay shapes is rather the opposite. Here a stiff sprig, perhaps a simple shape taken from a shallow sprig mould is beaten into a sheet of softish clay so that the sprig retains its outline but becomes flush with the surface, not proud of it (317). A brush of slip on one side will help the sprig to stick. The glaze can subsequently run into this outline picking out the shapes in an interesting way, or you can outline the decoration by staining with rubbed-on oxides.

Wrap-around slab pots can exploit both these techniques, and here you can also add reasonably damp clay simply by lying the pot on its side with a rolling pin inside, then rolling the wood round and over the pieces of clay. Coatings of sandy, groggy clays can be picked up in this way (which incidentally also thins out the walls of the wrap-around pot and interestingly elongates it) (319, 320).

All these ideas are even more easily accomplished with the press-moulded shape (111-113). You can lay out soft clay shapes on to a mould and place a sheet of clay over them so that they are pressed in easily (321); or place harder shapes on the mould – this time you will have to beat the sheet of clay gently over the shapes to integrate the two. Or all these techniques can be carried out the other way up if you are using the inside of the mould, putting the sheet of clay into the mould first, followed by the added clay. Remember that soft clay can be smoothed, smeared, or beaten on without keying and can then be incised and impressed with stamps and tools. Harder clay either needs slip, a roughened-up key, or both, to make certain it adheres – and usually is best left alone once it is on.

Staining

You can change the colours or tones of your work by using metal oxides to stain the clay you are using. They can be mixed in with the clay body itself to form a solid colour that goes all the way through, or you can apply them to the surface of the form only. First, however, you must

319 Paint slip on the wrap-around form while it is held on the 'former', in this case a thick round stick.

320 Roll the stick and pot over dried clay shavings, sand or grog to change the texture.

321 You can use clays of a different colour, rolled, cut, torn, directly on the mould, then cover them with a sheet of clay and beat the two together.

know your oxides, because they differ greatly: they may look alike unfired, but they vary a lot in strength and colour when fired. The main oxides are:

iron (various – red iron oxide, iron spangles, crocus martis); manganese; copper; cobalt; chrome; nickel; antimony and vanadium; rutile (titanium).

Body-stains (calcined, blended and refined oxides), can be bought from potter's merchants. Any reputable supplier's catalogue contains much useful information on body stains (they recommend using up to 15% by weight mixed into the clay), glaze stains, and the metal oxides that you can use alone or in combination to produce a whole range of colours for high and low temperatures. It is most important to remember that putting oxides into (or onto) a clay which already contains a fair amount of iron (such as red earthenware clay or even the pinky-buff or grey stonewares) will only result in a dulling or further browning of the body. You must use white- or light-firing clays if you want the oxides to show more of their full colour range, and then restraint is called for if you don't want rather garish colours. Getting the oxides into the clay is a messy business – iron, in particular, stains everything! Experiment first to establish quantities. If you are using the basic metal oxides, start within the limits for colouring slips on page 70.

You need patience in mixing to a thoroughly homogeneous state; I find the best way is to mix the oxide with a little of the clay and water so that it is creamy, slice the clay up; then 'butter on' the oxide. After this you must get your fingers and thumbs working on the mass of clay finally wedging and kneading until all streaks have disappeared. The only other way is to make the whole mass into a slip, sieve it, and then dry it off again to a plastic condition. These solid-stained clays can be used to make a range of decorative bodies (322-326). This kind of effect is called 'solid agate' (*colour 5*).

If you don't want a solid stain, then you might like to try staining only on the surface, simply by mixing up a thin solution of metal oxide and water, and painting, sponging, rubbing or spraying it on to the surface of the clay. These either burn away on the surface to give a close range of browns to greeny-blacks if left unglazed (it depends of course on what kind of clay you are using), or manifest their full range of colours if covered with a glaze. Opinions differ, but I prefer to apply oxides to the biscuit-fired pot so that not only can I clear away excessive staining with a wet sponge, but I also have much more flexibility as to how much concentration of oxide I build up. Some potters apply the stains to unfired clay, but then you must take care, when packing for a biscuit-firing, not to contaminate other work. Cobalt is so strong a stain that every finger mark will show. It is not very helpful here to give precise proportions of water to oxides because rubbing-on or painting-on build up different concentrations anyway. What must be remembered is the *relative* strengths of the oxides themselves. For example red iron oxide mixed with water can go on as quite a heavy pigment, certainly rather like a thin slip. Cobalt, on the other hand, will hardly stain the water or make a visible mark on the clay yet still it will give a light blue under a glaze. In between these you have copper which is quite a powerful oxide, and nickel, chrome and manganese which are less powerful. Make some small tiles, and rub in various mixes, try blending them too, and record carefully what you do and the results.

Impressions will hold the oxides to a certain extent and the textures and patterns will be enhanced by them. You can put glazes over the oxides but remember that some oxides have quite a strong fluxing effect (i.e. will make the glaze more runny) so experiment on small tiles etc before trying them out on a pot. You must make sure that the oxides are well rubbed into the body; if they remain as a dust on the surface, they could cause *crawling* (see page 101). And lastly you can mix the oxides into the glazes themselves (see 'Glaze').

322 Stain a clay with oxides or body stains and place in a pattern.

323 Squash them hard together to exclude any air.

324 Cut slices off the block and roll out to an even flatness before putting into or onto a mould.

325 Or knead the stained pieces into an arbitrary pattern.

326 Roll and prepare for the mould in the usual way.

Slip

Slip is clay softened by water to a consistency that varies from no more than a watery solution to a very thick cream-like condition. Metal oxides already present in the clays used to make the slip, or sometimes sprinkled but more usually sieved in with the slip, make possible a wide colour range. Slip was the main decorative method for many centuries before the advent of glaze. It is still used extensively by all potters whether working on earthenware or stoneware, handbuilding or throwing. Slips can be made from the white-firing clays, e.g. 50% ball clay, 50% China clay (these of course can be stained); or from the clay body you are working with, stained to give a contrasting colour; or from many of the red earthenware clays, e.g. the Etruria marls (which will stand quite high stoneware temperatures). All these can be applied to the raw clay, when it is in a soft to leather-hard condition. By altering the composition of a slip it can be made to adhere at the biscuit stage. The principle in the case of biscuit-ware is to substitute relatively non-shrinking China clay for the ball clay in the recipe and add some feldspar for a stoneware slip, or fritted lead or borax if a lower earthenware temperature is needed.

For example, Bernard Leach recommends (by weight): 6 parts China clay, 2 parts ball clay, 2 parts feldspar, which he used on high-fired biscuit tiles.

The pre-Columbian potters of South America, who never used a true glaze, nevertheless produced pots with smooth hard surfaces, highly decorated with marvellous patterns and motifs, all obtained by the use of naturally occurring or purposely stained slips (*365, back cover 4*).

Typical amounts of oxides needed to colour slips

Remember that the more iron in the clay to start with, the duller the colour will be. All the non-iron oxides will give their brightest colours in white slip. The type of glaze you will use to cover the slip will also affect its colour.

Red iron oxide	2%-10%	tan to dark browns
Manganese dioxide	2%-8%	light to darker brown-purples
Copper oxide	2%-5%	various greens
Cobalt oxide	$\frac{1}{2}$%-$1\frac{1}{2}$%	light to strong blue
Vanadium stain	6%-10%	yellows
Rutile	4%-8%	creamy tans
Iron chromate	1%-2%	light greys

Combinations of oxides

Red iron oxide 2%, plus cobalt oxide 1% gives grey-blue.
Red iron oxide 3%, plus cobalt oxide 1%, plus manganese dioxide 3% gives black.

You can apply slip to a thrown pot as soon as it is made – indeed brush-banded decoration done in a freshly-made dish or on a pot is simple but often very effective. When you have brushed the slip onto the wet clay surface, with the wheel still turning you can incise a pattern of lines and areas through the slip, or you can paint some more slip of another colour on as well. You must choose the right moment to apply your slip at the various stages – apart from painting on the wet, thrown pot, slip usually goes on in the soft to leather-hard state by painting, pouring, or dipping. Remember that slip contains a very high proportion of water, and that water softens clay and ultimately might soften it to such an extent that the pot will collapse, handles fall off tearing the wall away with them, and plates and press-moulded dishes crack across before the water has the time to evaporate away. If all this sounds like a disaster area you must

327 Incise through the slip coating before it gets too dry, use a wooden comb, or bevel-ended tool or piece of bamboo.

not worry, because slip, once understood, is really the kindest of masters and will change the colour, texture and even visual proportion and balance of your work for you. There is moreover, in high fired ware, a reaction between the surfaces of clay, slip and glaze which gives a unique depth to the fired pot. Certain guide-lines are worth remembering:

1 Unless a dish or bowl is dry enough to take slip (i.e. leather-hard) – but not so dry (i.e. it has changed colour) that the slip will flake off – then see that the form is supported, for example thrown plates and dishes are best slipped *before* they are turned when they are still thick.

2 If your work has handles or other thinner additions then you must make sure that they are firm enough to be slipped – the rest of the form may have to be kept damp while these pieces dry off a little. Conversely there may be a time when handles etc. will have to be wrapped up in a thin, slightly damp cloth, to stop them from drying too much. It all depends on the work and the state of the clay.

3 Soft to leather-hard forms seem to take slip best; once they have started to change colour around the edges some slip might not adhere to them.

4 White slips, or those stained ones based upon white slip, crack off more easily than do iron-based slips (stained or not), so try to get them on while the clay form is damper than usual. If bad cracking or flaking occurs then the slip recipe must be adjusted, (possibly by using more ball clay in the recipe).

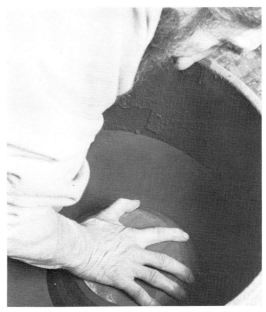

329 Dip a large form in slip, with one hand in the slip holding the rim of the vessel the other pushing down on the base.

330 Bring the pot out of the slip and hold for a moment to allow drips to run off.

328 Stoneware store jar with incised and sgraffito decoration by Michael Casson.

331 Swiftly draw the sponge across the wet slip, speed is essential, the slip dries quickly.

You can use slip to enhance the effects of all the previously-mentioned techniques carried out before biscuit-firing: incising through slip is called sgraffito (327, *328*); you can impress into slip, or slip can go over the top of impressions. Areas of slip can be used to contrast with lines and areas of inlay; slip-coated forms can be pierced (it is better to coat with slip first, because slip added after piercing may weaken the form and cause it to collapse); clay can be added on top of slip, (it helps it to adhere); a slip-coated form will make it easier to pick up sandy clays, grogs, dry clay shavings, etc., which you may want to use to give texture to the surface of handbuilt forms.

You can paint slip on, pour it over, or dip the form into it. This is the time when you can swiftly sponge, finger, or comb patterns in it when it is still wet from application (329-331, *colour 12*). You can also build up layers, providing you let each coat go leather-hard; the work of Elizabeth Fritsch is notable here among young contemporary potters (*colour 15*).

Wax and paper resist

There are two other interesting methods of decorating with slip which use the contrasting tones or colours of the body and slip to get a decorative effect, namely wax and paper resist; both stop the slip from entirely coating the form. Bernard Leach is a master of both of these methods, while Hamada has specialised in the hot wax technique to decorate his work.

Wax resist

The traditional way of 'stopping out' a pattern by using the wax resist method is to melt a mixture of paraffin wax until it is quite runny and to paint it on to the unfired clay quickly, before the wax sets. Then the pot is dipped immediately into slip, or slip is brushed over the wax to break and splatter in an interesting texture where it runs off and gathers on the underside of each brush stroke. Small drops of slip that remain on the wax are left by the potter as accentuating dots and splashes in the wider brush strokes (332-335). This, or variations of it, is still the most exciting way to resist a pattern with hot wax. The method is the same whether you are using a thin mixture of oxide and water to decorate with (best painted, not dipped), or thick glaze on a biscuited pot. You may have to alter the thickness of the waxy medium for the latter but the procedure is the same. I use a heated mixture of candles and light machine oil. I cut up the candles and cover them almost completely with the oil and find that this proportion is all right for most slips. Thick glaze may need more candles to resist it while thin oxide and water mixtures will need more oil. In this way I can easily regulate the effect. I wait until the mixture is good and hot – even smoking slightly – before I paint or trail it on the pot. Today you can also buy a cold emulsion which you simply shake up each time before you use it (337-339, *back cover 6*). It is more easily controlled and has the added advantage of not damaging your brushes, but I feel it takes away some of the excitement from this lively method which for me could affect the spirit of my work.

Paper resist

Whereas wax resist can be essentially a fast, almost nerve-wracking method calling for split-second decisions on pattern-making, cutting or tearing paper to form your decoration is slower, more painstaking and capable of many adjustments before the slip is applied. Bernard Leach recommends the use of Japanese rice paper for all paper-resist work (*336*), but this is difficult to get now, and I have found that wet newspaper works well. You simply prepare your paper pattern by cutting or tearing the paper into shapes and, when the clay is still leathery, smooth it into position on the surface. Some potters damp the clay and sponge the

332 Heat the wax over a stove, quick decisive brush strokes work best with hot wax.

333 After the brush-stroke pattern has been built up dip the whole pot into slip.

334 You can encourage the slip to break on the wax by a gentle shake.

335 The whole pattern will quickly emerge.

336 Large pot with paper resist and painted decoration by Bernard Leach.

337 Alan Caiger-Smith paints design on bowl with wax – includes a vegetable dye (which burns away) to show where strokes have been made.

338 As soon as emulsion is dry, band over bowl with metal oxide, using wide flat brush.

339 Alan sometimes leaves an unpainted 'lost line' on the way, which binds pattern together around the bowl.

paper over; I prefer to soak the paper, shake off the excess water and stick it firmly on to the pot, sponging it down if it shows a tendency to rise. I find that it is easiest to build up a pattern in smaller pieces of paper rather than to attempt a complicated lace-like structure that easily breaks up when wet. When the design is complete dip the pot in slip, or paint slip over it, and don't be in a hurry to peel the paper away. I usually leave this until the next day, when I pick off the paper with a pin (340-342). Once the first coating of slip has dried off slightly, more damp paper can be smoothed on and another coating of a different coloured slip applied to give varied tones and colours when the work is finally glazed and fired.

340 Place wet paper shapes onto the dampened surface of the pot, sponge over if necessary, they must not lift up at all.

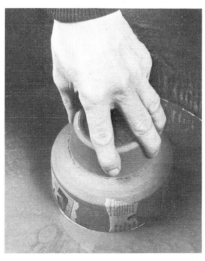

341 Dip into slip.

342 When the slip is leathery, peel away the paper.

Burnishing

A plain clay surface can be smoothed and compacted by rubbing with a hard object like the back of a spoon, a bone or a pebble when the leather-hard state has been reached. Some very early pots were decorated in this way until the decoration stood out as quite shiny areas. The full potential of this very controllable technique is realised when slips are painted on and burnished to give contrasting areas of smooth bright colours, as the pre-Columbian potters of South America did before the Spaniards introduced the lead glaze. It is laborious work painting and burnishing, but the results can be spectacular. Low-fired ware, below 1000°C, seems to retain the burnishing best and many good burnished pots have come from simple sawdust kilns. John Ablett has made maximum use of burnishing – look at his intricate work (343), and Sheila Fournier's sawdust-fired dish shows what can be done by simple means (396). But so far very little experimentation has gone into producing higher-fired burnished pots.

343 Bowl by John Ablett, slip-painted, unglazed and burnished earthenware.

Slip trailing

Of all the ways of applying slip to obtain a pattern or a decoration on clay the most traditional way in Britain has always been with the slip-trailer (344, 345). This tool, made in bygone days from a vessel like a baby's feeding bottle with a reed in one end and the user's mouth at the other end to control the flow, produces lines, dots, even small areas of varying thicknesses according to the size of the reed or nozzle opening. There have been slip-trailers made of fired clay, bags of cloth or rubber, syringes and cake icers, in fact anything that will give a steady spread of slip that can be stopped and started at will. You can buy them too, of course. I favour a rubber ball or bag with glass nozzles of varying sizes to give thin and thick lines. English 17th century and 18th century slip-trailed dishes such as those made by Thomas Toft, and pots like the lively

344 Slip-trailers.

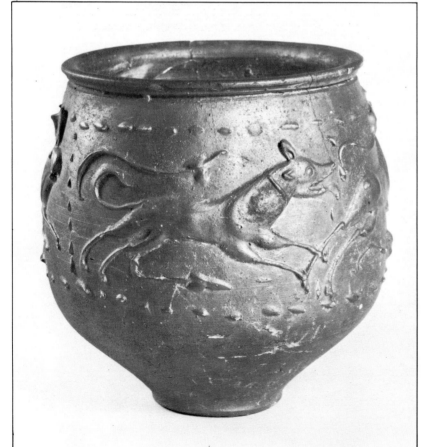

345 Gallo-Roman earthenware cup with slip-trailed decoration, 2nd century AD.

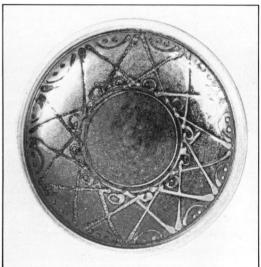

346 Dish, slip-trailed, high temperature wood-fired earthenware by Peter Dick.

Staffordshire posset pots, have never been equalled (*347*). They speak of bucolic humour, of peasant traditions in a pre-industrial age; perhaps this is why so few potters now can use this fine method with real flair and conviction. Peter Dick in Yorkshire is one of these few exceptions (*346*).

The technique itself requires practice in every department. First the slip itself must be well sieved so that no lumps impede the steady flow. Picking up the slip into the trailer, so that no air is taken in, is a minor art in itself. The experienced slip-trailer must know just how stiff the creamy mixture must be to trail freely across the surface of the work; this will differ for different occasions. So you must practise, at first on rolled-out flat slabs of clay so that confidence is built up before a curved dish or actual pot wall is tackled.

As well as the line, dot, and small area of slip in all the variety of slip colours available, the slip decorator can produce many other surface decorations by using a 'ground' or coating of wet slip on which to trail. While the dish or pot is still wet from the poured or dipped slip ground, thick and thin lines of a different slip can be quite arbitrarily trailed on and the whole work gently shaken about so that the two slips twist and slide around to give a *marbled* effect (*348*). More controllable all-over decorations are produced by trailing parallel lines of slip over a wet slip ground and carefully drawing a fine point across these lines to give a *feathered* appearance to the surface. Combining some of these methods, for example, with combing or sgraffito, show how rich a vein of decoration slip is.

347 Slip-trailed plate by Thomas Toft, lead-glazed earthenware from Staffordshire, early 17th century.

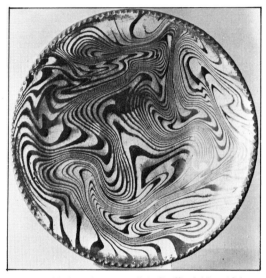

348 Marbled earthenware dish, Staffordshire, 18th century.

The brush

There seem to me to be two main ways of using a brush: as a tool for delineating and/or filling in areas with slip, metal oxide and even glaze, and as an expressive medium in its own right. Both uses have resulted in some fine decoration. For example, the Mediterranean world of Minoan and Greek potters produced brush-painted work using lines and areas that was lively, strong, exciting – even in some of the painted Attic figures, serene (*2, 349*). The pre-Columbians too used the brush to paint, in slip, their complicated decorations (*424*). But the shape, spring, 'quality' of the brush played little part in these pots except insofar as they were the right size and type for the job. It was drawing with the brush rather than painting with it. The difference between each brush inherent in its material and shape is seen at its best when we look at Far Eastern pottery (*1*) and at certain Islamic pots of the Middle East (*104*). Using a brush to write with from childhood has given the Eastern potter a facility denied to others, and certainly the brushwork patterns we see on Chinese and Japanese ceramics, whether abstract or representing, as they more usually do, something from nature, are without rival. Only some Hispano-Moresque dishes (*colour 13*) or painted Kufic or Naski (*418*) letters can be considered beside them. Oriental painting uses the brush *stroke*; the brush, the wrist and the arm perform their actions to achieve the desired result.

All brushes, as Alan Caiger-Smith points out, have a language of their own. You can use Western brushes from the sign writer's trade as well as Oriental brushes and others specially designed for making particular strokes. Any brush will leave a characteristic mark – and leave a distinctive shape round the mark (*350-353*). Alan Caiger-Smith also stresses the use of positive and negative shapes that brush strokes make and leave; the way they are chosen to enhance a particular curve, the patterns they make as the strokes repeat and build up, and the counterpoint of the marks of one brush against another – broad and short against thin and long – is the way he sees his decoration (*357-363*).

349 Minoan Vase, 13th century BC, an example of throwing with added coils of clay thrown on; the octopus has been painted in iron-bearing pigment on the unglazed earthenware surface.

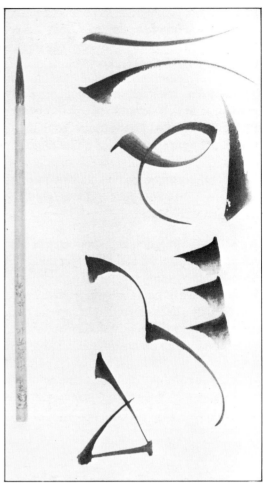

350 Japanese brush – very supple; line tends to go from thick to thin; good at curves; has an 'informal' and a 'formal' edge.

351 One-stroke signwriter's brush – 'if you can handle big brushes you can handle smaller ones'.

He says: 'There really is no general recipe: it is all too individual. But there are some useful maxims which apply to most things.

1 Get to know the pot, its curves, their changes, the rim, the texture, ridges, and so on. Whatever marks you make are going to be affected by these things, and ideally you will have fashioned this form with the 'decoration' in mind. Some shapes don't need decorating at all; some are very difficult. The more you are aware of the form as a whole, the wider your options and the more you can choose the placing of a design, the scale, the relation between different parts. When one feels there is no choice, it's usually because one has not yet taken in the form. Really see the form and it begins to talk to you. Even if you paint only on a part of the form, those marks still belong to the form as a whole.

2 Be true to the original idea. If the feeling comes through, a lot else takes care of itself. Is the design overall or localised? Dense, involved, mysterious, or free and open? Static, or moving? Does it reach out, or is it quiet and composed? Keep true to the character, and most of the details will sort themselves out.

354 Alan Caiger-Smith runs the Aldermaston Pottery, where he works with a team of 8 potters. He is renowned for his brush-painted maiolica, and for his lustre-ware, which is achieved by subtly-controlled wood firing. He has exhibited in the UK and all over the world, including Japan.

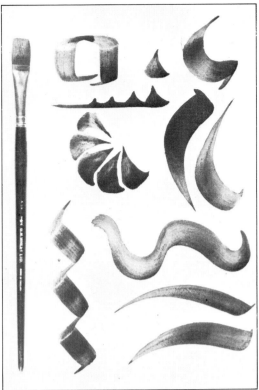

352 Small signwriter's brush.

355 Goblets by Alan Caiger-Smith painted with various oxides over a white tin glaze.

353 Fine-point brush.

3 Make friends with your brushes. Whether you paint an O or an ostrich, you work through the natural movements of a particular brush, and each brush has its own repertoire. It is helpful to try them out first on flat paper, then with water or dye on an unfired pot. Try out the same stroke at different speeds. Try different handgrips, and remember that you can move yourself as well as the pot. Notice what you leave out as much as what you put in.

4 Paint thick to paint thin. Every colour has its own ideal thickness, impossible to describe. One has simply to remember what was done and compare it with the fired result. Here, as with brush movements, it is usually helpful to start strong and refine the result, rather than to begin weakly and try to strengthen it.

5 Real decoration has heart; the rest is only a substitute. It begins in unexpected moments; in fields or streets, in dreams, in laughter or sadness. It is only *carried out* at the work-bench.'

356 Brush-painted bottle, high-fired stoneware by David Eeles.

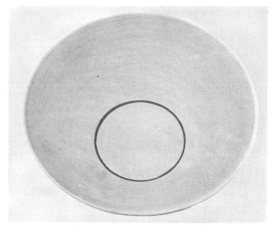

357 A line using small Japanese brush accentuates change of form where bottom of bowl becomes the side.

358 Big signwriter's brush – 3-movement angled stroke – note doubling-up effect where brush changes direction.

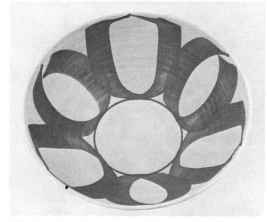

359 Same brush – contrast with a round stroke – note where it cuts or overlaps the stroke before.

360 Fine brush gives a light, dancing stroke.

Other potters use a brush more to represent nature, like the plant forms that David Eeles uses on his work (*356*). Eric Mellon with his circus ladies (*colour 8*) and Elizabeth Fritsch with her fractured strata of lines and areas (*colour 15*) make the brush subservient to their design conception. Either way the brush is a major tool of the decorator's art. Find out what you can get from each brush by practising on newspaper – it has a similar absorbency to a pot.

When to paint
A few practical points on the various stages at which you can paint will save time and disappointment; but no-one can tell you the actual strength of the slips, oxides, etc., that you want, you must record your findings and build up a palette of colours that you can repeat.

(a) *Painting on the raw clay* with slip or oxides and water presents few problems because the unfired pot absorbs the moisture readily and the brush work will be fired on to a certain extent in the biscuit kiln; you can get rid of mistakes more easily and you can also scratch fine lines through the pigments as an added interest.

(b) *Painting on the biscuit-fired pot* under the glaze on the other hand is prone to come off as the glaze is applied (by pouring or dipping), so it is as well here to mix in a little gum arabic with the oxides. Simply grind up a little gum (about 2%), with the powdery oxides on a tile or piece of glass, add the water and paint on as you would water-colour paint. If you use too much pigment the glaze will crinkle or crawl over it, too little will just not show up. You can buy all these from potter's suppliers as well as other specially prepared colours that are calcined and ground mixtures of oxides, fluxes and sometimes clays and binders as well.

(c) *Maiolica painting:* pigments on the unfired surface can smudge when you handle the pot before it is finally fired; underglaze colours may not give you the desired depth of colour, so you may choose to paint with oxides *on top of unfired tin glaze* (tin glaze fires opaque white). This can give you a stronger colour, but can present more problems because the powdery glaze is extremely absorbent, like blotting paper, and tends to come away with the brush stroke (354, *355*). Here again, gum arabic or gum tragacanth, in the glaze this time (about 2%, but you will have to experiment), will help to make a harder surface to paint on. But I have found that timing is the most important factor in Maiolica painting. If the wet shine has gone off the glaze surface you can paint rapidly and surely with oxides and water, and perhaps a little gum and/or glaze. I only leave ten to fifteen minutes after glazing (depending on the hardness of the biscuit firing or thickness of glaze) before I paint with oxides (or wax-resist).

If you paint or wax too soon the strokes will disturb the glaze; if too late the glaze will either lift off then or it will bubble or crawl under the painting, because in this powdery state it absorbs too much water. Alan Caiger-Smith uses a cold wax emulsion (stained with a vegetable dye, so he can see where he has painted), when painting his Maiolica decoration (*back cover 6*). Then he bands on his pigment, over the wax, with a brush. Underglaze painting was used by the Islamic potters, especially in conjunction with the brilliant turquoise glaze so characteristic of Persian and Egyptian work of the 12th century. Tin-glaze painting was first used by the Middle Eastern potters, then taken over by the Europeans – Italians (Maiolica), French (Faience), and Dutch and British (Delft); in some of these countries the technique is still used in the traditional way.

(d) *Overglaze enamels* and *lustres* are highly specialised techniques: the brush is used to paint them on to the already fired glazed surface; both need lengthy experimentation to produce good results. Unlike all the other painting methods you are not dealing with oxides or even blends of oxides simply mixed with water. *Enamels* are really low-firing glazes, whilst lustres need special kiln control to give their best quality. They need special preparation, blending, calcining and grinding if you are to make them yourself. Both can be bought commercially, however, and most suppliers will give information on their use. They need a third firing to a low temperature from 600°C-900°C to fix them on to the surface of the work. The Japanese have long been masters of enamel firing and Hamada and Leach working in our own time have mixed their own pigments to paint on their stoneware and porcelain. The 12th century Persian Minai painters were able to use the miniature paintings of the time as a source of inspiration (*colour 14*). The palette they used was stunningly varied, red, brown, purple, grey and black used alongside gilding and even over cobalt and manganese underglaze painting as well. This kind of control and discrimination is rare among our studio potters today and the very wealth of colours you can buy ready-made from the suppliers spells danger; technical facility does not always make for good pots. The application is really a question of coming to grips with the relative thicknesses of the various pigments as they are supplied, most will have to be mixed with an oily medium before painting on to the fired surface; some might come ready mixed with this medium. You will have to learn by your mistakes how thick or thin each colour can be used. Be guided by manufacturers' recommendations.

Lustres employ metallic salts fused on to the surface of the work in a third firing (biscuit and glaze). True reduced lustres, certainly the subtlest, richest kind, need a heavily reducing flame to produce the best results. They emerge from the firing blackened by smoke and have to be

361 Japanese brush – the 'dagger' stroke, a tricky one.

362 Whole arm moves in a stroke which draws design up to rim.

363 A little rolling stroke – brush drier – to break formality of base circle.

cleaned to reveal their colour. Alan Caiger-Smith and more recently
David Eeles both use this traditional method to give the rich range of
colours to their work. Alan, using a wood-firing kiln, has long been the
acknowledged master of this difficult and often frustrating medium
(*colour 11*). Bought lustres industrially prepared with resins that give the
'local' reduction to the metals need an oxidising firing to about 600°C.
They are effective but not to be compared to the reduced lustres first used
by the Islamic potters of Egypt (*364*), and brought to the height of
artistic achievement in 12th century Persia and Spain during the
Moorish occupation (*colour 13*).

364 Bowl from Egypt, tin-glazed earthenware with a Coptic priest painted in gold
lustre, 12th century, signed by Sa'd the potter.

365 Press-moulded stirrup-pot, Mochica pre-
Columbian Peru, painted lobster decoration
7th century AD.

The beginner is often overwhelmed by the enormous range of decorative
methods available. I have not even mentioned the industrial or semi-
industrial methods of 'printed' decoration, ranging from rubber stamps
dipped in fluid oxides – which certainly can be used easily by the artist-
potter – to silk screen, engraved and lithographic transfers, and
photographic techniques which certainly cannot be used without
sophisticated equipment. If any guidelines at all are to be laid down, I
suppose the best advice is to start simply and small scale. Take one, or
perhaps two tools only – cutting tools, brushes, etc. – at a time. Use one
oxide only and get to know its range by using it sparingly at first,
increasing to a more full-blooded application as confidence mounts.
Look at the best examples you can find in museums, galleries, books. It is
an area full of pitfalls but offering rich rewards in terms of expressive
fulfilment.

Glaze

PART I MAKING A GLAZE
by Lynne Reeve

Potters glaze their work for a number of reasons: with a glaze, the craftsman can give his pot any texture, colour and decorative effect that he chooses. The use of glaze is particularly important in the case of functional ware since a faultless, smooth glaze provides the pot with a hygienic covering – and in the case of a porous body, such as some earthenware, glaze also makes it waterproof.

The development of glazes, though sometimes regarded as a difficult and mysterious subject, can in fact be very straightforward. Even if you decide to buy a ready-made glaze, you will often want to modify it to suit your own requirements. You may not be familiar with some of the chemical names used here, but all the ingredients are commonly occurring minerals, and can be obtained from a potter's supplier. Technical terms are explained in the Glossary.

What is glaze?

Glaze is basically glass which has been melted onto the surface of the clay, and is made up of a number of minerals. These raw materials, which are collected in rock form, must be ground before use to a fine powder. When applied to the clay without any addition and fired, most of the materials produce dry 'immature' (that is, not fully melted) surfaces which bear no resemblance to true glazes. But if we can carefully select two or more different raw materials and mix them together in certain ratios, when fired, these will produce 'mature' (that is, fully melted) glazes. An understanding of this fascinating interaction of materials is the basis of ceramic glaze making.

Composition

As a general rule, all glazes for all firing temperatures need three essential ingredients: these are silica, flux and alumina.

Silica

Silica is the main constituent of glass. It occurs naturally as flint and quartz. Sand is an example of a crystalline form of quartz, and flint is often found in the form of pebbles or large nodular flint stones. Silica will melt if heated to 1700°C and then cool to form a glass. However, most of the clays used to make pots can only withstand temperatures of about 1300°C or lower, so silica alone cannot be used as a pottery glaze: something must be added to it, so that a glassy material can be formed at a lower temperature. This additive is called a flux.

Flux

There are large numbers of fluxes; each has a different 'fluxing' or temperature-lowering strength, and each will give the glaze a different surface quality – the choice of flux in a glaze is determined as much by the quality given by the flux as by its fluxing power. Many glazes are named after the principal flux used in the recipe: for instance, we speak of dolomite glazes and magnesium glazes. Low temperature glazes need more powerful fluxes than do high temperature glazes. So initially the fluxes will be divided into two categories: 'Stoneware fluxes' for use at 1200°C and over, and 'low temperature fluxes' for use at temperatures below 1200°C.

---

366 **WEIGHTS AND SIZES**
All unturned unless stated.

The clay body ie its composition, wetness, firmness;
the method of making eg thrown, thrown and skimmed, thrown and turned;
the shape eg wide flat base, small base and swelling form;
all of these and of course the skill of the potter have a bearing on the final size the thrower makes with a given weight of clay.
Here are some typical shapes with the weights of clay it takes to throw them:

Cylinder

Weight	High	Wide
1 lb	5″	4″
·4536 kg	12·7 cm	10·16 cm

Bowl

Weight	High	Wide
1 lb	3″	6″
·4536 kg	7·62 cm	15·24 cm

Mug

Weight	High	Wide
10 oz	4″	3½″
·2835 kg	10·16 cm	8·89 cm

Store jar

Weight	High	Wide
10 oz	3½″	3″ (opening)
·2835 kg	8·89 cm	7·62 cm
lid 5 oz ·1417 kg		
Weight	High	Wide
1¼ lb	5″	3¾″ (opening)
·567 kg	12·7 cm	9·525 cm
lid 7 oz ·1984 kg		
Weight	High	Wide
2 lb	7″	4″ (opening)
·9072 kg	17·78 cm	10·16 cm
lid 8 oz ·2268 kg		

Flour bin (NB: 9″ wide flat base)

Weight	High	Wide
4 lb	7″	5″ (opening)
1·8144 kg	17·78 cm	12·7 cm
lid 1½ lb ·6804 kg		

81

(a) Stoneware fluxes

Whiting (which is powdered chalk), dolomite and magnesium carbonate are three examples of fluxes used in high temperature glazes. These and many other high temperature fluxes tend to follow a set pattern of behaviour: small additions of 5% or 10% to a glaze tend to increase the shine, larger quantities make the glaze matt – in fact many potters use this method of making matt glazes. It is a general rule that the larger the number of different fluxes used together, the more powerful the fluxing effect: thus 20% of a single flux is usually less effective than 10% each of two different fluxes. The use of several fluxes in one glaze also has the effect of increasing the firing temperature range of the glaze.

(b) Earthenware fluxes

There are a few fluxes which when fired alone will melt a glaze at very low temperatures of 1000°C and below. Three of these are boron, lead and colemanite (whose chemical name is calcium borate). Unfortunately each of these is unsuitable for use in its naturally occurring form. Boron is soluble in water (water-soluble materials are difficult to use); lead is highly toxic and soluble in weak acid even after firing; colemanite, depending on its source, presents various problems in use, crawling (a defect which is described later) being the most common. So it is necessary for these fluxes to be processed before they are used in glazes. All these problems associated with solubility and instability can be overcome by combining the flux with silica. These silicate materials are known as 'frits' and the process of combining the flux with silica by heating the two substances together is called 'fritting'. These frits can be bought from a potter's supplier. Almost always a certain quantity of one or other of these special fluxes will be needed to produce a glaze which will melt below 1200°C. High temperature fluxes can also be included in low temperature glazes, and they can add interesting qualities, but the quantities used will have to be small, usually below 10% for glazes firing at 1050°C and lower; more for glazes maturing above 1050°C.

We now have two components in the glaze recipe: the glass-forming silica and some flux. By choosing the appropriate flux, we can form a glaze which will melt at any temperature between about 800°C and 1300°C. Unfortunately the glaze thus formed will be rather unstable and inclined to run; it may even flow off the pot and onto the kiln shelf. So we need one more ingredient.

Alumina

To give the glaze stability and adhesion we can add a substance called alumina, which is found in several minerals: for example in the feldspars (sodium feldspar, potash feldspar and calcium feldspar), and in the lithium compounds (lepidolite, spodumene and petalite). Inclusion of any one of these materials can provide a sufficiently large content of alumina for some glazes. For more generous additions however, powdered clay can be used since it contains a particularly large percentage of alumina. Additions of powdered clay, as well as stiffening a runny glaze, will of course also make the surface less shiny.

These then are the three essential parts of a glaze recipe: silica the glass-former, fluxes to lower the temperature at which the silica-glass can be formed, and alumina to stabilise the glaze. Now we can consider the proportions in which these materials are to be used. For this purpose stoneware and earthenware glazes must be considered separately.

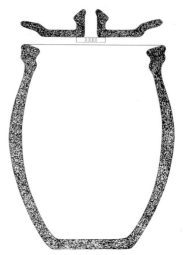

Bread bin (NB: 14″ at widest point)

Weight	High	Wide
20 lb	16	10½″ (opening)
9·072 kg	*40·64 cm*	*26·67 cm*
lid 5½ lb	*2·4948 kg*	

Jug

Weight	High	Wide
14 oz	5″	3½″
·3969 kg	*12·7 cm*	*8·89 cm*
½ pint	*·284 litre*	
Weight	High	Wide
1½ lb	7″	4″
·6804 kg	*17·78 cm*	*10·16 cm*
1 pint	*·568 litre*	
Weight	High	Wide
2¼ lb	9″	4½″
1·0206 kg	*22·86 cm*	*11·43 cm*
2 pints	*1·136 litre*	
Weight	High	Wide
4 lb	11¼″	5¼″
1·8144 kg	*29·21 cm*	*13·335 cm*
4 pints	*2·272 litres*	

Plates (turned)

Weight	High	Wide
1¼ lb	1¼″	7″
·567 kg	*3·175 cm*	*17·78 cm*
Weight	High	Wide
3½ lb	1½″	11″
1·5876 kg	*3·81 cm*	*27·94 cm*

The proportion of ingredients

Stoneware glazes

These are glazes which are applied to iron-bearing, white or porcelain clays and fired between 1200°C and 1300°C and sometimes higher. It is very easy to make a stoneware glaze because there are some minerals which in their naturally occurring form contain all three of the constituents needed. The most widely used of these minerals are the feldspars – silica, the fluxes and alumina in feldspar are in the correct proportion to form the basis of a stoneware glaze, and luckily for potters, feldspar is one of the most commonly occurring minerals on the earth's crust. If for instance the potash feldspar rock is ground to a fine powder, mixed with water, passed through a fine 120 mesh sieve, applied to biscuited clay and fired to 1250°C, the result is a glazed surface. However, this glaze made from potash feldspar alone is imperfect for functional ware; its irregular and slightly pitted surface shows that it has not flowed sufficiently, some more flux is needed. The best way of discovering the quantity of flux needed to give the necessary degree of flow, combined with the required surface texture, is to take the stoneware fluxes one at a time and try several small additions of them to the basic feldspar glaze. For example: the following tests, using potash feldspar and whiting, give a considerable amount of information about the behaviour of these two materials.

Potash Feldspar	Whiting	Result
95%	5%	Lacks flow, pitted
90%	10%	Fairly shiny
85%	15%	Good
80%	20%	Immature, pitted
75%	25%	Immature, pitted

The result of these tests fired to 1250°C, show the recipe 85% potash feldspar + 15% whiting to be a particularly successful glaze. It is shiny, with an even, smooth surface.

Ash glazes

Another material which contains all the essential ingredients for a glaze, though not always in the correct proportions, is ash. Ash as a glaze ingredient can be derived from any combustible material – woodash, and ash from straw and grasses are the most popular among potters. The composition of ash varies greatly: there is even a seasonal difference in the chemical composition of the wood of a single tree. Almost all ashes contain silica, alumina and a large number of fluxes. The amount of silica in an ash may be anything from 2% to 80%. The silica content is critical since it largely determines the 'hardness' of the ash: a very siliceous ash will have a very high melting temperature, an ash which is low in silica will usually fuse (that is, melt) at a lower temperature. Some ashes will produce beautiful glazes without any addition whatsoever. Others may require up to 70% or 80% of additional materials such as clay and feldspar.

Preparation of the ash: Some potters wash the ash several times by soaking it in water, then sieving the mixture through a coarse sieve (about 40 mesh). They may repeat this procedure four or five times. The washing process removes the soluble salts from the ash and often produces a better-behaved glaze. But there are also potters who argue that the washing removes some interesting qualities of the ash. They prefer simply to sieve the ash, dry, through a coarse sieve to remove the largest particles. Once prepared, the ash, if wet, should be dried. It can then be weighed out in the same way as the other glaze ingredients.

4 cup Teapot

Weight	High	Wide
1½ lb	4½″	2¾″ (opening)
·6804 kg	11·43 cm	6·985 cm

round shape lid 5 oz ·1417 kg

6 cup Teapot

Weight	High	Wide
2½ lb	5½″	3½″ (opening)
1·134 kg	13·97 cm	8·89 cm

round shape lid 8 oz ·2268 kg

Cup and Saucer

Cup (turned)

Weight	High	Wide
9 oz	4″	3¼″
·2551 kg	10·16 cm	8·255 cm

Saucer (turned)

Weight	High	Wide
12 oz	1¼″	5¾″
·3402 kg	3·175 cm	14·605 cm

Casseroles (turned)

Weight	High	Wide
3 lb	5″	8″ (opening)
1·3608 kg	12·7 cm	20·32 cm

lid 1¼ lb ·567 kg

Weight	High	Wide
5½ lb	6″	10″ (opening)
2·4948 kg	15·24 cm	25·4 cm

lid 2¼ lb 1·0206 kg

Weight	High	Wide
8 lb	6½″	12″ (opening)
3·6288 kg	16·51 cm	30·48 cm

lid 3 lb 1·3608 kg

Before experimenting with additions to the ash, always fire a sample of the ash alone at the required maturing temperature. This will establish whether the ash is 'refractory' (that is, resistant to high temperature) or low-melting, very fluid. A dry ash will require the addition of feldspar or a flux; ash which fires to a glassy glaze may require additions of clay or talc.

Although many ashes have a maturing temperature in the stoneware range or higher, they can be used to good effect in earthenware glazes, though the quantities used in the low temperature recipe may have to be lower than in the stoneware glazes. Anyone wishing to experiment with ash glazes cannot do better than refer to the notes in Bernard Leach's *A Potter's Book*, which are taken from the research work of Katharine Pleydell-Bouverie.

Earthenware glazes

The feldspar base used for stoneware glazes is too refractory for earthenware temperatures. It is more suitable to use 'frits' as the basis for low temperature glazes to which you can then add the other ingredients as you would to the stoneware feldspar bases. One point of difference however, is that these frits might initially require some stiffening from clay, probably about 20%, rather than an addition of flux.

The concept of the 'base glaze'

The mixture 85% potash feldspar, 15% whiting is an example of a 'base glaze' recipe. A base glaze is one which can be added to, and thus altered, to produce a number of new glazes. This particular glaze lends itself so successfully to variation that it is very often used by potters as the common denominator for a wide range of glazes. The base glaze does not have to have such a simple recipe – it can be any glaze which is used as the starting point for further experiments, and its composition influences the effect of any addition made; this is why one 'blue' glaze, for instance, may turn out to be greyish-blue and another greenish-blue, even though the same quantity of identical blue colouring agent may have been added to both glazes.

Additions to the base glaze

By adding one or two ingredients, the base glaze can be changed in a number of ways. It can be (i) made more opaque or even totally white, (ii) given colour and (iii) made more or less shiny.

(i) Opacity

An opaque glaze is one which totally obscures the original colour of the clay body. The colour of the clay can be seen through the transparent base glaze of 85% potash feldspar + 15% whiting, but it is possible to make this glaze opaque by adding what is known as an 'opacifying agent'. There are several materials which come into this category; the most commonly used are zirconium silicate, tin oxide, zinc oxide and titanium dioxide. These materials produce opacity either by remaining for the most part undissolved in the glaze melt, as in the case of tin oxide, or by forming crystals in the glaze, as in the case of titanium dioxide. Apart from making the glaze more opaque each of these materials gives a different surface quality.

You can vary the degree of opacity by using different amounts of opacifier. Amounts of about 10% give a milky translucency, and approximately 15% of any opacifier is required to make the transparent base glaze totally opaque at a firing temperature of 1250°C. If you add more than the quantity you need to produce a completely white glaze,

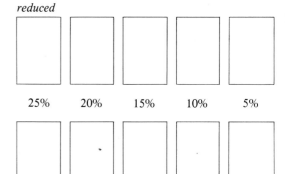

OPACITY Key to tiles, colour photograph 19

Recipe:
Base glaze (85% potash feldspar + 15% whiting)

+ ZIRCON

reduced

25%	20%	15%	10%	5%

oxidised

COLOUR Key to tiles, colour photograph 21a

Recipe:
Base glaze (85% potash feldspar + 15% whiting)

+ COPPER OXIDE

	7·0%	
	5·0%	
	4·0%	
	2·5%	
	1·5%	
	0·5%	

oxidised   *reduced*

pinholes or crawling may result. (These are defects which will be described later.) Very small amounts of opacifier, on the other hand, act as fluxes in the glaze: up to 5% of zinc oxide, for example, can give a beautiful shiny finish to a glaze which is already fairly shiny but uninteresting. In a very glassy glaze it is sometimes necessary to add very large quantities of opacifier, even as much as 25% or 30% before any opacity is obtained, because the glaze is so fluid that it dissolves the crystals or particles of opacifier. Since opacifiers are generally more expensive than the clay or feldspars you may find it helpful in the case of such fluid glazes to add about 5% of China clay in order to lessen its fluidity, then smaller quantities of opacifier will be effective. The procedure for opacifying both earthenware and stoneware glaze is the same, except that you will need less opacifier in earthenware glazes (*colour 19* and key).

(ii) Colour

Certain metal oxides will give colour to a basic, colourless glaze, but bear in mind that the colours obtained from a single oxide can vary considerably depending on the type of atmosphere present in the kiln during the firing (see page 95, *oxidation and reduction*) (*colour 21* and key).

Iron oxide

This oxide gives a range of yellows and browns in an oxidised firing, and blue-greens, olive-greens, browns, blacks and reds in reducing atmospheres. The blue and green glazes are known as 'celadons' (*colour 9, 301*), the richer brown and black glazes made with iron are called 'tenmokus' (*colour 7, colour 12, 367*). Small additions of iron to a glaze tend to make it more shiny, but larger quantities make the glaze matt due to the formation of iron-silicate crystals. Amounts of iron oxide added to the basic recipe can vary from 0·5% up to 25% or even more. The most mysterious colouring effect of this oxide is the beautiful 'Chun' blue glaze, where a colourless glaze of special composition derives its hue from the low iron content of the body or slip to which it is applied (*colour 2*).

367 Plate with wax resist decoration by Bernard Leach.

COLOUR Key to tiles, colour photograph 21b

Recipe:
Base glaze (85% potash feldspar + 15% whiting)

+ COBALT OXIDE

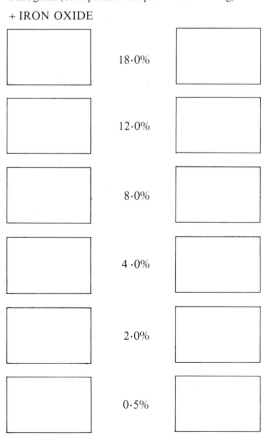

oxidised		reduced
	2·0%	
	1·5%	
	1·0%	
	0·5%	
	0·3%	
	0·1%	

COLOUR Key to tiles, colour photograph 21c

Recipe:
Base glaze (85% potash feldspar + 15% whiting)

+ IRON OXIDE

oxidised		reduced
	18·0%	
	12·0%	
	8·0%	
	4·0%	
	2·0%	
	0·5%	

Cobalt oxide

Cobalt oxide gives a range of blues, light to dark. Very small quantities of this oxide are required as it is an extremely powerful colouring agent – in fact a single grain of fine cobalt oxide, if allowed to contaminate a white glaze, will show as a violent patch of dark blue on the white glazed pot after firing. The quantity of cobalt oxide required to make a shiny glaze pale blue is only 0·1% and for a dark blue just 0·8% to 1% is needed. (Slightly larger quantities of cobalt oxide however can be used in matt base glazes.) The colours given by cobalt oxide are much the same in reducing and oxidising atmospheres (*back cover 5*).

Copper oxide

The colours obtained from copper oxide vary greatly according to the kiln atmosphere. In oxidation, the colours will range from pale yellowish green to dark green and metallic black (*colour 6*). In reduction firings, the same quantities give a range of pinks, reds and metallic black (*colour 10*), although the reduced copper red glazes are unreliable; they tend to vary from firing to firing and are sometimes broken up by areas of green. Amounts ranging from 0·5% to 8% can be added to the shiny base glaze. The volatilising behaviour of copper oxide is such that it affects the colour of nearby pots in the kiln during firing and often leaves coloured deposits on the kiln shelf even in low temperature oxidised firings.

Manganese dioxide

Manganese dioxide gives a range of purples and rich browns. The colour you will get depends on the composition of the base glaze. Amounts of over 25% in a shiny base will sometimes give beautiful lustrous glazes of brown and amber in either reduced or oxidised firings. Unfortunately, there are problems associated with the use of large quantities of manganese dioxide as it is inclined to make the glaze runny and it sometimes causes bubbling.

These and other less commonly used colouring oxides can be added to either an earthenware or a stoneware base, the same considerations apply. The actual quantities required at the two extremes of temperature are surprisingly similar although the colours you will get in the fired glaze tend to be brighter and clearer in earthenware glazes, since there is less interaction with the clay body, which tends to have a muting effect on the colour of stoneware glazes.

It is important generally to note that the metal oxides also act as fluxes in the glaze, though this effect is not noticeable if very small quantities are used.

The first table on p. 87 shows the effects obtained by adding these colouring oxides to the base glaze of 85% potash feldspar + 15% whiting. All the glazes are fired at 1250°C. The second table shows the average strength of some colouring oxides. Information in this table applies to both stoneware and low temperature glazes.

(iii) Mattness

The word 'glaze' implies a shiny covering, but you can also get a range of delightfully subtle effects, from a satin sheen to the dry, earthy surface quality of stones and pebbles (*270, 328, 368, 417*).

One method of making a glaze matt is to add powdered clay to the basic recipe. The addition of clay is in fact merely increasing the maturing temperature of the glaze. An attractive brown matt glaze can be made by taking one of the iron-coloured glazes already mentioned (85 parts of potash feldspar + 15 parts whiting + 10 parts iron oxide) and adding 10 parts of powdered china clay. Another method of making a glaze matt is to use a large amount of one of the stoneware fluxes, such as whiting or

Table (i) Colouring oxides

Recipe		Results	
		Oxidised	*Reduced*
85% feldspar + 15% whiting	+ 2% iron oxide	yellow shiny transparent	light green shiny transparent
— —	+ 10% iron oxide	brown shiny translucent	brown shiny opaque
— —	+ 20% iron oxide	dark brown matt	reddish brown matt
— —	+ 0·1% cobalt oxide	light blue shiny	light blue shiny
— —	+ 0·6% cobalt oxide	dark blue shiny	dark blue shiny
— —	+ 0·5% copper oxide	pale yellowish green shiny	pink shiny
— —	+ 3% copper oxide	strong green shiny	red shiny
— —	+ 4% manganese dioxide	patchy brownish pink	brownish yellow
— —	+ 6% manganese dioxide	pinkish brown	light yellowish brown
— —	+ 10% manganese dioxide	rich dark treacle-like brown	mid-yellowish brown
— —	*+ 12% manganese dioxide	rich dark treacle-like brown	dark yellowish brown

* This and larger quantities of manganese dioxide begin to make the shiny base glaze runny in both reduced and oxidised firings.

(Figures given for colouring and opacifying additions to the glaze apply specifically to this base glaze of 85% feldspar: 15% whiting, and will not necessarily be directly applicable to all other base glazes. The figures can however be used as starting points for experiment.)

Table (ii) Table of average strength of colour in glazes

Colourant	Oxidised	Reduced
cobalt ½-1%	blues	
iron 1-10%	yellows, rusts, browns, blacks (greens and blue-greens)*	
copper 2-5%	greens	reds
manganese 2-6%	plum to brown depending on glaze and temperature	
iron chromate 1-4%	greys	
vanadium stain 4-10%	yellows to yellowish greens	
rutile 2-10%	tans, and also to break up or mottle other colours	

* Yellows, rusts, brown to brown/blacks can be obtained in oxidised and reduced atmospheres. The greens and blue-greens can only be obtained in reduced atmospheres and when the proportion of iron is comparatively small, i.e. 1%-3%.

dolomite. While we know already that small amounts of these materials will make the glaze more fluid and shiny, further additions will gradually make the glaze more matt. So we can also make the brown glaze above matt by increasing the amount of whiting, so that the recipe becomes: 85 parts potash feldspar + 25 parts whiting + 10 parts red iron oxide. In addition to the stoneware fluxes, another particularly useful material which can be added to glazes to give a smooth matt surface is talc (ordinary talcum powder) which contains the flux magnesium oxide as well as silica; between 5 and 20 parts is usually enough.

All these matting agents can be used in stoneware or earthenware glazes, but less than half the quantity used for stoneware matt glazes is sufficient for an earthenware glaze.

To add to the range of possibilities various effects of colour, opacity and mattness can be used simultaneously. Interesting and beautiful glazes can for instance be made by adding colour to an opacified glaze. The results here can be particularly rewarding since the opacifiers have a pronounced modifying effect on the colours. A good example of this is the following stoneware glaze, fired at 1250°C in a reducing or an oxidising atmosphere: 85 parts potash feldspar + 15 parts whiting + 5 parts titanium dioxide + 5 parts iron oxide; this gives a dramatic dark blue speckled glaze.

The use of powdered clay in a glaze

Apart from the matting property of clay already mentioned, there are other advantages in including clay in a glaze recipe. Chemically, clay provides the glaze with both alumina and silica. In clays other than the pure white china clays, a number of fluxes and some metal oxides, usually iron, are also present. These substances can of course be supplied by other minerals, so it is not essential for a glaze to contain clay, but the presence of clay makes for easier use of the glaze in its raw state for the following reasons:
(a) It improves the suspension of the glaze in the bucket.
(b) It gives strength to the dry raw glaze on the pot. This means that the glaze is not too powdery before firing and is therefore less likely to be knocked or rubbed off the pot. The more plastic the clay, the greater the suspension and strength given to the glaze. High plasticity is also associated with a high shrinkage rate, so very plastic clays should be used cautiously or crawling may result.

The high shrinkage of a glaze is essential, however, if the potter is raw glazing (see page 94) because the glaze must accommodate the unusually high shrinkage of the clay (the shrinkage of 2 normal firings takes place, in this instance, during one firing). You may need to use as much as 50% of normally plastic clay in a raw glaze, though in the case of an exceptionally plastic clay, such as some ball clays and bentonite, as little as 15% may be enough. These are sometimes called 'slip-glazes'.

There are several categories of clay which can be used in a glaze:

China clay

China clay is the least plastic of the clays (in fact it is not sufficiently plastic to be used alone as a shrinking agent in a raw glaze), but it does aid the suspension, and increase the raw strength of the glaze. It is a white clay free of impurities, and will therefore not discolour white glazes or cause any speckling. It is more refractory than iron-bearing clays so it is also a stronger matting agent.

Ball clay

Ball clays are very plastic and are therefore very useful as glaze ingredients if used in moderate amounts. Most ball clays contain

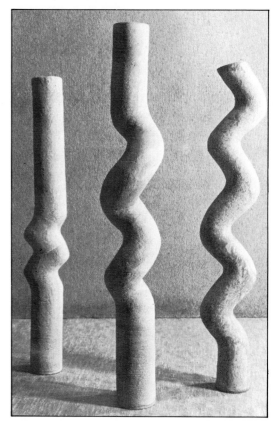

368 Handbuilt stoneware pipes, matt ash glaze by Gillian Lowndes.

369 Salt-glazed teapots with reduced copper decoration by Mary Rich.

particles of iron which cause speckling·of the glaze in reduction firings and a yellowing of the glaze in oxidised firings.

Red earthenware clay
The addition of red earthenware clay provides a plastic ingredient for the glaze and at the same time a fairly large quantity of red iron oxide.

Local clays
Locally dug clays, if carefully sieved and dried before use can often prove to be uniquely interesting additions to a stoneware or earthenware glaze. As well as giving plasticity to the glaze, they provide a complex combination of minerals which often give unusual colours and surface qualities of a richness that can rarely be imitated by laboratory-determined mixtures.

Bentonite
Bentonite is the most plastic of clays, so much so in fact that just 0·5% or 1% in a glaze will give adequate suspension of particles. In amounts of over 5% the bentonite gives a gelatenous quality which renders it unusable.

370 Stoneware teapot with fluted decoration by David Leach.

Clay body and kiln atmosphere
The mineral content of a glaze, as outlined above, is obviously the most important aspect of glaze making. There are however two other factors to be considered, which always have a major effect on the appearance of a fired glaze.

(i) The clay body
The colour and the texture of the simplest base glaze is dependent on the composition of the clay body of the pot to which it is applied. A single glaze is therefore capable of great variation in appearance. A glaze on porcelain, for instance, will have a smoother surface and clearer colour than the same glaze on a rough-textured, buff-coloured clay. A semi-transparent white glaze on a buff body, for instance, will become yellow and dull in an oxidised firing and pale green in a reduced stoneware firing. Both these effects are due to the presence of the small quantity of iron which is also responsible for the buff colour of the clay. The effect of the colour of an earthenware clay body is not so great since there is less interaction of clay and glaze at low temperatures. A red earthenware clay will obviously be clearly visible through a transparent glaze, but the more subtle effects of speckle and slight discolouration of the glaze on a buff body rarely occur in opaque earthenware glazes.

371 Salt-glazed teapot by Sarah Walton.

(ii) The kiln atmosphere
The type of firing (see page 95), has several effects on the glaze, the more obvious are as follows:

(a) If the atmosphere is oxidising, i.e. oxygen-rich, the glaze appearance will be fairly clean and bright since impurities in the clay will not greatly influence the glaze. Under reducing conditions however, where the amount of oxygen in the kiln is greatly diminished, there is greater interaction of clay and glaze and any impurities in the clay will show as speckles in the glaze.

(b) The actual hues themselves given by the colouring oxides are often very different if reduced as opposed to oxidised during·the firing.

(c) In the reduction firings, as a result of the oxides returning to their metal state, lustrous qualities can be obtained from special glaze composition; such effects are rare in oxidised firings.

372 Porcelain teapot with incised decoration under a light celadon glaze by Terry Bell-Hughes.

Preparing a glaze

Particle size

All the required materials can be bought in fine powder form from the various suppliers. If locally dug clays and rocks are to be used these must be crushed and ground to a powder and should pass through a 120 mesh sieve to ensure good interaction of materials. A very fine particle size results in more thorough combination of ingredients and thereby in a more readily melting glaze. There are occasions however, when the inclusion of larger particles is an advantage, as in the case of some ash glazes and some heavily speckled glazes.

Weighing the ingredients and mixing the glaze

The powdered ingredients should be carefully weighed. Colouring oxides, especially the strong ones such as cobalt oxide, should be weighed on a very sensitive and accurate balance. After weighing, mix water with the powder until you get a creamy consistency. (It is advisable to wear a mask during the mixing of the glaze, as the fine powder tends to become airborne.) When mixing strong colouring agents into the glaze it is a good idea to grind them together with a few spoonfuls of the base glaze in a pestle and mortar before adding them to the rest of the mixture and finally sieving the batch of glaze. Most glazes should be put through a 120 mesh sieve (a coarser mesh, about 40, may be needed for ash glazes). For very thorough mixing of the glaze, the sieving process can be repeated.

The glaze is now ready for use. The thickness of the glaze is important. There is a simple rough and ready guide for finding the correct consistency of the glaze: dip a dry finger into the glaze and out again fairly quickly. If you cannot see the outline of your finger then the glaze is too thick; if you can see the colour of your finger through the glaze then it is too thin. The shape of your nail should be discernible through a totally opaque layer of glaze. The hydrometer (374) is more reliable!

Suspension of the raw glaze in the bucket

When the glaze has been mixed it can be stored indefinitely but it must always be thoroughly stirred before use. Some glazes will require very little stirring to bring the glaze back to an even consistency. Other glazes tend to settle into a solid mass at the bottom of the bucket leaving almost clear water above. These poorly suspended glazes tend to be those which contain little or no clay. An addition of clay, if this can be made without spoiling the fired glaze, will solve the problem. The more plastic clays give greater suspension: an addition of just 0·5% or 1·0% of bentonite, which is the most plastic of all clays, is usually enough to suspend the heaviest of glazes.

In less severe cases of a settling glaze, a few spoonfuls of vinegar in the bucket will be helpful.

PART II GLAZE APPLICATION

The first glazes we know about seem to have been invented by the ancient Egyptians who mixed the glaze ingredients into the clay body, so that by evaporation the glaze came to the surface. It was a chancy business and often resulted in patchy effects. Many hundreds of years later in Medieval Europe the raw lead that was the basis of the glaze was probably shaken on to the unfired pots as a dry powder from a cloth, as was the copper that gave the rich speckly green so characteristic of the pitchers from the middle ages (191). Today's artist-potters prefer to *dip*,

373 Salt-glazed teapot by Peter Starkey.

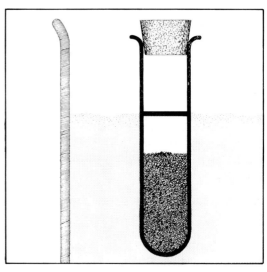

374 Using a hydrometer.

pour or *spray* the glaze, usually onto a biscuit-fired pot; in each case the glaze is first made into a liquid by suspending the powdery non-soluble ingredients in water.

To determine which method of application to use you must ask yourself certain questions. Can your pot be held easily so that you can dip it into a bucket? Have you enough glaze to cover it, or should you pour the glaze over it? Is your work of such a character, perhaps very delicate or intricate, that the runs and pouring marks that can come by dipping or pouring will spoil the finished effect? Or perhaps even the sheer size of the work means that spraying is the only answer? Potters often make a virtue of the way they apply glaze: vigorous throwing marks accentuated by runs from a dipped glaze; a large flat wall of a slab-built form made more interesting by a flood of poured glaze that gives different tones where it doubles over itself.

Whichever way you choose there are some basic hints that are helpful:

1 Always dust or clean with a damp sponge all work about to be glazed; dust can cause pin-holed glazes, or worse, even crawled bare patches.

2 Always stir the glaze well to an even mixture and keep it stirred all the way through a glazing session. If a pot is very thin it is quite a good idea to glaze the inside first and let the pot dry thoroughly before dipping or pouring the outside, otherwise the thin, saturated walls will not pick up the outside glaze, resulting in a mean coat of glaze on the outside of the pot.

3 The higher the temperature to which the pot has been biscuit-fired the more difficult it is to apply glaze, and some potters put gum in the glaze to help it adhere to the high-fired clay. Earthenware often has to have a first firing well over 1000°C to prevent undesirable crazing, but stoneware and porcelain can be biscuited at a much lower temperature, usually 950°C or even lower, so the trouble here might be sucking up *too much* glaze. Adjustments can be made by making the glaze thinner or thicker in the bucket with more or less water before the glazing session begins. A device that will help you measure the thickness of the glaze is easily made by partially filling a small glass tube or old metal cigar container with sand; hold it in the stirred glaze and continue adding sand to the tube until it floats *upright*; mark the glaze line round the tube and cork it (374). Next time you use the glaze see to it that the tube lines up at the same place.

What I do is always take some water off the top of the glaze (the thicker glaze ingredients always settle to the bottom of the bucket), then stir it up adding back just as much water as I think I need for the particular hardness of my biscuited pots and the aesthetic effect I expect from a thin or thick glaze.

Of the three main ways of applying glaze, dipping and pouring are the simplest and most economical on glaze, and most commonly used by the artist-potter.

Dipping

Bernard Leach describes in his great work *A Potter's Book* the way pots are glazed by the flop-dip method, but it requires practice and has its limitations on size and the shape of the work being glazed. Most potters take the pot in one hand and a jug or dipper full of glaze in the other, swill the *inside* with glaze, tip out the excess and follow in with the pot to cover the *outside,* dipping right up to the fingers holding the pot at the base (375-378). (When you fill your bucket with glaze, allow for displacement – remember Archimedes!) If you have planned your pot well in the first place you can get a firm grip on the footring or at the base. You must hold the pot level, as you dip it in upside-down, to prevent the glaze getting in,

375 Fill the mug with glaze.

376 Pour out.

377 Hold level and dip in up to fingers.

378 Pull out slowly and hold for a moment to allow glaze to settle.

379, 380, 381 Dipping a plate, the feet have been waxed so that the whole plate can be immersed in the glaze. As you put it down, slide the fingers swiftly round the rim to disperse the wet glaze, and paint on more glaze later if necessary.

then air pressure will prevent glaze getting up inside the pot; the whole operation must be swift and sure so that too much glaze is not sucked onto the porous clay surface. Sometimes you will not be able to hold the work upside-down, so you may find that a coating of wax (cold or hot) on foot-ring or across the base will mean that you get a different hold or grip around the top (379-381), allowing you to dip into the glaze base first without getting glaze on the foot; you must avoid glazing the foot of a stoneware or porcelain pot, because it is placed directly on the kiln shelves. You can dip large or awkward pieces first one way and then the other but remember that most glazes, especially opaque ones, will show the overlap if two coatings are allowed to form (382-390).

382 Fill $\frac{1}{4}$ full with glaze.

Pouring

Here it is almost impossible to avoid double coatings with run and pour marks but they can be made a decorative feature of the work. I would suggest that with more experience you think ahead from the making stage to the glaze application stage so that you plan this kind of feature on your work. Pouring is usually done by resting the upturned pot or work on two thin sticks over a container to catch the excess glaze (391). The stick marks must be painted in or touched up with glaze later. Bases can be waxed to prevent the unnecessary build up of unwanted glaze there and the glazer usually pours round the piece rapidly until the pot is covered. Drips on the rims and edges of poured pieces often give trouble, because they either set quickly and might have to be scraped down, or if cleared away leave a raw rim. Here I prefer to clear the drips away and paint the glaze on the edge. Painting glaze on is another way of applying glaze but few potters now use it although Lucie Rie probably could not get some of her special effects by any other method (*colour 17*).

383 Roll the glaze round away from the spout up to the rim of the teapot.

Spraying

There certainly may be very good reasons for spraying glaze but you must remember that this method could mean a large outlay of money. Small amounts of thin glaze, or oxides and water, can be sprayed on, using a mouth-blown spray or scent spray, etc., but for larger amounts a proper spray-gun with compressor and spray booth with extractor fan (to suck out the fine particles not adhering to the work) are necessary (392). Both are costly items. If you have to spray, then the points to remember with spraying are: keep the right distance with the spray gun so that wet runs of glaze do not appear; do not allow the work to get saturated; and clean the apparatus on completing glazing, otherwise

384 Pour waste glaze out of spout. Blow down spout to clear filter holes.

385 Dipping (i) – wax *rim* of teapot, finger over spout to stop glaze going up into pot.

386 Withdraw slowly and hold.

387 Dipping (ii) – wax *base*, thumb on spout to prevent glaze running in.

388 Dip up to rim, see that all the spout gets covered.

389 Pour glaze onto the lid.

390 Pour away excess glaze, clean the rim of the lid immediately, the base of the lid is glazed later. The whole of the rim, top and underneath, is left unglazed so that it can be fired on the pot.

there will be trouble next time. Certain shaded effects can only be achieved by spraying and it can be a great help in glazing large raw-fired work, or delicate, complex porcelain forms, otherwise I would say that dipping, pouring and even painting are economically and aesthetically better methods in most cases.

Remember to make tests, putting one glaze on top of another, possibly using different application methods – for example a poured or painted glaze on top of a dipped one. Exciting results can come from this and greatly increase your glaze repertoire.

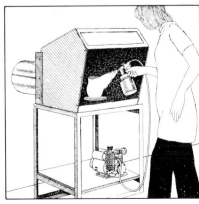

392 Spraying-booth with fan, compressor and spray- gun.

391 Pouring – the pot rests on stout wire, the base is waxed.

Fire

We fire pottery to make it permanent because even clay baked hard by the sun can be rendered down and used again by crushing and mixing with water. But once the clay has fired to approx. 600°C then the chemical and physical changes that occur make the irreversible change from clay to pottery.

This progression from clay form to hard and durable pottery must take place slowly, because water, whether the 'atmospheric' water surrounding the clay particles, or 'chemically combined' water (i.e. combined with clay at a molecular level), must be driven off slowly if it is not to vaporise and burst the walls of the pot. Leave large pots and thick clay objects to pre-heat and dry out thoroughly on a shelf over a firing kiln. Potters usually fire pots twice; one is called the biscuit firing, the other the glaze firing. This is not essential (and historically 'biscuit' came in rather late in the day, generally speaking not until the 17th century).

However, some potters still like to fire their pots once only and leave out the biscuit stage; this is called raw firing. This method has the advantage of saving time and fuel. It does however, mean that the pot must be glazed when it is still unfired and very fragile, so quite a high level of knowledge and expertise is necessary. You will need to pack the kiln as for a glaze firing (page 95). In the early stages of a raw glaze firing (i.e. up to 600°C), the temperature must be increased gently while the water is driven off, just as in the case of a normal biscuit firing. Once the kiln has reached 600°C the firing can be continued like a normal glaze firing on and up to the high temperatures needed to melt most glazes. In fact the potter is merely telescoping the two separate cycles into one. When using this method the potter needs a glaze with high shrinkage properties (see pages 88, 95). (Industry usually fires to a much higher biscuit temperature than the glaze fire – in order to get rid of certain glaze faults, especially crazing in earthenware.)

However, biscuit ware is easier to handle for glaze application and certain decoration processes.

393 Packed biscuit kiln.

Kilns

Kilns are fired with anything that will give heat. Fuels from camel dung to solar energy have been used successfully but the most usual are wood, coal, oil, gas and electricity. The last is certainly the easiest, although more expensive, and small kilns of about one cubic foot (0.029m³ approx) which run off a 13 amp supply can cost around £150. Historically, kilns probably started as just fires lit under and around a heap of dry pots (potters in Papua and West Africa still fire this way). As soon as holes in the ground or sections cut into banks of earth were used higher temperatures became possible. The simple bottle-shaped up-draught kiln, where the heat simply travelled up through the ware and out through the top of the kiln, served the Western potter for centuries, but in the East the down-draught kiln, which allowed heat to build up as the flames were drawn down through the work and out through the chimney at the back of the kiln, meant that much higher temperatures could be reached. Today sophisticated fuels like oil, gas and electricity serve the latest technology that, for example, uses alumina and silica spun into blankets or compressed into boards with which to make kiln walls.

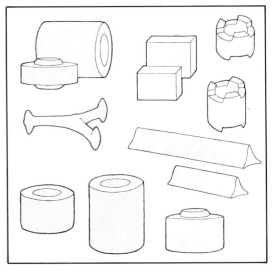

394 Kiln furniture – props, spurs, stilts, connecting pieces.

Oxidation and reduction

The potter is confronted with the choice of two atmospheres, *oxidation* and *reduction,* inside the kiln. The two kiln atmospheres have a crucial bearing on the final appearance of the work. Oxidation means firing with adequate air to allow good clean combustion. In reduction, the kiln is starved of air by adjusting the air intakes and flues. If the combustion is to continue, it must take oxygen from somewhere, and so if it cannot draw it in from outside the kiln, it will take the necessary oxygen from the oxygen in the clays and glazes. This results in the iron-bearing stoneware clay bodies turning warmer and speckled in a typically reduction-fired look, and an alternative colour response from many of the other minerals used in the glazes. Electric kilns (unless fitted with silicon carbide elements) do not take kindly to a reducing atmosphere, whilst wood and coal are not easy to handle, especially at the high temperatures. So it seems sensible to settle for the very extensive range of effects that an oxidising atmosphere can give from an electric kiln, or use gas or oil to achieve reduction. Potters have very different firing cycles, but in my own case, after 6 hours firing, I give my gas kiln 6-7 hours reduction, starting at 1000°C, up to 1260°C, when I re-oxidise for 15-20 minutes to reach 1280°C.

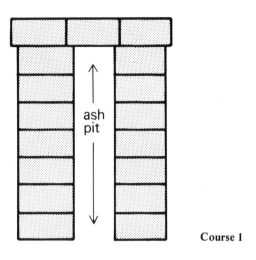

395(a) Plans for simple wood fired kiln built on flat compacted earth or on concrete
1st course, ash pit, firebox; chamber floor, 5 similar courses for chimney fire box door.

ash pit

Course 1

Packing and firing a biscuit kiln

As there is no glaze to melt and stick the pots together, and as the pots will eventually shrink by about one tenth in the firing (the overall shrinkage of wet to final pot is more like one eighth, or greater in the case of porcelain), they can be packed inside and on top of each other and can touch at any point (393). There is a very slight expansion before the shrinkage begins so pots should not be wedged tightly together, and a small gap should be left at the sides and especially at the top of the kiln. (Pots should not touch electric elements.) The best way is to pile the pots up carefully, the strongest at the bottom supporting the lighter ones. 'Bungs' or columns of pots can reach from the floor to the roof of smaller kilns. Ceramic shelves can be used to pack delicate things on, or for shapes which do not fit well together. Whatever your fuel, start the firing slowly; do not allow the temperature inside the kiln to build up by more than 100°C in any hour, even less with very large pots. Build up gradually until you can see a good red heat (around 700°C) then proceed more rapidly until the firing is completed (around 950°C for stoneware and porcelain; usually you should fire earthenware higher, say to 1000°C). The best safeguard you can have is really bone dry pots to begin with. An average size small electric kiln of 15″ × 18″ × 20″ (38 × 46 × 51 cm) can take up to 12 hours for a biscuit firing, depending on the size and thickness of the ware.

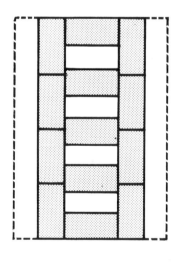

**Course 2
Fire box
floor**

Packing a glaze firing

Here the melting glaze will stick pots together or onto the shelves – which must be used to separate the ware – so leave a small gap about $\frac{1}{4}$″ (1 cm) between every pot, and dust shelves with powdered alumina to soak up any glaze that falls. In stoneware and porcelain glaze firings, the bases of the work must be left unglazed, but in earthenware the pots must be glazed all over if they are to be waterproof; so place earthenware pots on specially made ceramic pieces, stilts, spurs, etc., which lift them off the shelves (394). These spurs leave razor-sharp marks that you must grind down later, with a carborundum stone. Special care must be taken with the thinner, more delicate porcelain pieces; setting them absolutely level on even, flat shelves will help to stop distortion. All shelves should be supported on three props set out in a triangle and each set of props holding a shelf must be directly in line with the ones underneath. If more

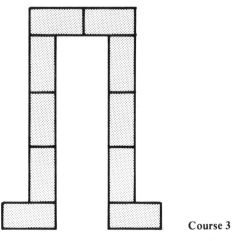

Course 3

than one tier of shelves is used then the shelves in one column should be staggered higher or lower than the next one, so that the heat can flow easily through the kiln and not be shut off by shelves lying at the same level right the way through the kiln; this can cause gross over- or under-heating and ruin your work. An average electric stoneware kiln can take up to 14 hours to fire and reach 1250°C. Methods vary, but as a general guide, start with the power on *low* for a couple of hours, then up to *medium* for 3 to 4 hours, then on *full* until you reach your required temperature. Some potters using electric kilns learn to play their dials like some musical instrument, holding the heat back at top temperature to give them the special effect they seek. Every potter develops an ideal firing procedure that is right for a particular kiln – and potter! Some potters revel in the fact that their kiln took only 4 hours to reach temperature, others love staying up all night nursing theirs along – highly individual people, potters . . .

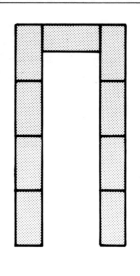

Course 4

Recording temperature

Electric devices – pyrometers – can be bought for measuring the temperature inside the kiln, or you can use specially made 'cones' of compressed materials similar to those used in glaze making. They are made to melt when they reach predictable temperatures, and you can buy a whole range of cones to suit any temperature requirement. We usually use three or four cones in a row, one designed to melt before the temperature required, to give a warning, one to melt at a hotter temperature so that when it remains standing we know we haven't over-fired. As the temperature may vary from one part of the kiln to another we often use a couple of rows of cones set in different parts of the kiln in front of the spy holes in the kiln door. This way we have warning of under- or over-heating.

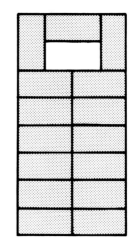

**Course 5
Floor of firing chamber
Lay this course over a kiln shelf**

Lastly, when the kiln has fired and starts to cool down, do not be in too much of a hurry to open up and see results. In stoneware and porcelain it helps to let the temperature drop very rapidly just after the firing has ended by opening all the bungs or fire-box doors, but when the kiln really is getting cool, that is the time to avoid cold air getting in to crack the pots inside. Complicated changes are taking place in the clay body from approximately 600°C downwards, and the kiln should be left undisturbed until below 200°C, when it can be opened up, bit by bit.

Making your own kiln

While electric, gas, oil and high-temperature wood kilns make considerable demands on the expertise of the kiln builder (for those so dedicated or committed there are books and articles on these, see Booklist), there are two very simple types of kiln that can be built in your back garden and yet produce subtle or spectacular glaze results for you. They are
The sawdust kiln particularly good for small pots decorated at the raw clay stage, and especially for the burnished or slipped and burnished pot; and
The low fired earthenware wood kiln suitable for melting lead or soft borax frits and especially for Raku, the Japanese ware for so long connected with the tea ceremony and all the arts contained in that religious rite.

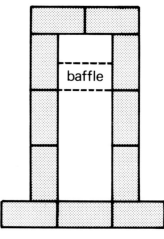

baffle

In courses 6, 7, 8 use some unbonded bricks (next to the spy hole) and half-bricks as a removable door to firing chamber

Course 6

Sawdust kiln

This really is simplicity itself; built out of house-bricks and protected with a metal dustbin lid it will last a long time (397). Probably it will reach a temperature of only about 800°C at the most. But it is sufficient to change clay to pottery, and burnished pots can become quite tough when fired in a sawdust kiln. Just light the *dry* sawdust at the top of the kiln,

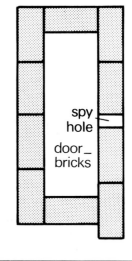

spy hole

door bricks

Course 7

396 Pinched and burnished bowl by Sheila Fournier, very low fired in a sawdust kiln.

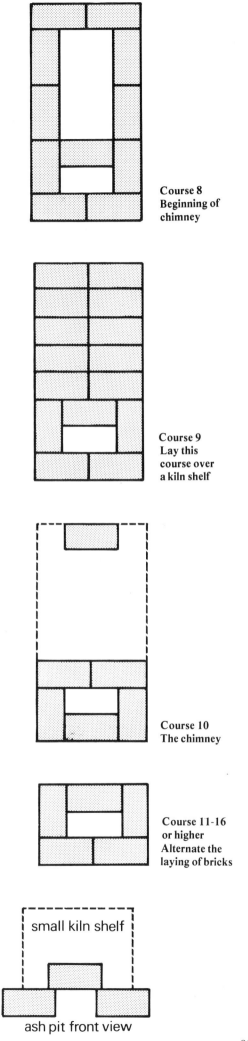

Course 8
Beginning of
chimney

Course 9
Lay this
course over
a kiln shelf

Course 10
The chimney

Course 11-16
or higher
Alternate the
laying of bricks

small kiln shelf

ash pit front view

replace the lid and let it burn *downwards*. Open it next day or when it feels cool, but be careful, it can still be quite hot. The best type of clay for this is a rather fine-grained earthenware red clay, or one of the smooth stonewares offered in all the catalogues from pottery suppliers. Remember that the pots must be bone dry before they go into the sawdust, and as you can see from the diagram the open-mesh chicken wire keeps them separated and prevents them all collapsing into a heap after the firing. Burnishing, impressing, painting-on of slips and oxide stains are all highly successful in sawdust firings (*396*).

Low temperature wood-fired kiln

With under 200 house-bricks you can build a small wood-firing kiln that will reach 800-900°C in a short time, about 2-3 hours. To begin with build the one in the diagrams (395a); later you can make the more advanced one with a door (395b). Raku ware was made traditionally in Japan from coarse clay so that the pots could be lifted, hot and glowing, straight out of the kiln and plunged into leaves or sawdust or straight into water without blowing apart. They may crack, but as they were about to be used for a tea-drinking ceremony and were considered expendable this did not matter. It is still a good idea today to use a heavily grogged or sanded body – say 25%-30% or more to start with, later more refined clays can be used if you wish, when you have more experience. Pinch pots and simple modelled pieces work well with this clay. They must be thoroughly dried (many Raku potters place their work on top of the firing kiln to heat them up), before they are low, biscuit-fired (800°C). The glazes used on these low-fired wares rely on lead or borax frits (which can be bought ready-made) to melt at the low temperatures required (*colour 18*). Bernard Leach has described the whole process in several books and there are now many publications dealing specifically with Raku (see Booklist).

A good supplier's catalogue will give you plenty of information. If you go on to use the normal metal oxides you will soon build up a repertoire of glazes, clear, opaque and coloured. Don't forget that Raku glazes are thickly applied for best results. Start by trying the following recipe:

100 parts of a low-firing frit, e.g. borax or lead frit, melting at about 900°C, (many have a range from 800°C to 1050°C), plus 10 parts China clay.

These two ingredients will melt and give you a clear glaze in your Raku kiln. Then you can add 5 to 10 parts whiting and/or 10 parts tin – this gives a lovely, opaque white.

Then you can add the colouring oxides, for example 4 parts copper oxide is quite spectacular because you have the added possibility of oxidising or reducing the pots as they come from the kiln: you can either plunge them straight into water to oxidise them, in which case any copper, for example, will go green, and any clay body showing will remain light; or you can roll them or cover them in some organic combustible material like leaves, grass, sawdust, peat, etc. In this case not only will the oxides give their reduced metallic colours (the copper will go red), but also the exposed body will blacken dramatically, contrasting with the highly crackled glaze and oxide colouring. It is a spectacular type of firing that really demands great control to bring out the best results, but happily gives an absorbing pleasure while you are learning.

As well as the bricks for the kiln you will need a stout pair of asbestos gloves and some long tongs for removing the pots from the kiln. Old dustbins to hold the leaves, sawdust, etc. and one for water are also advisable for Raku firing (398). And of course once you begin to master your kiln, Raku is not the only type of low fired pots that can be fired in it. Earthenware with fritted lead glazes fired in the usual way (i.e. bring them up to temperature, let the kiln cool down, then remove them cold from the kiln), is just as possible using wood in this firebox, but in this case the bricks should be set in a rough fireclay and sand mixture; in fact the more you insulate it with mud and ash, and use fire bricks (possibly even two layers of them), the higher the temperature will climb in the small chamber where the pots are (but remember that common house bricks won't stand very high temperatures, much over 1000°C). You must split the wood into thin, long pieces and it *must* be dry. The more you do this the quicker the whole firing cycle will become. Wood is probably the most exciting fuel potters use, its crackle, smoke and flame appeal to the elemental in us. Many kilns will be too difficult to build or use for the beginner but this plan and sketch should enable you to start experiencing the effects of real fire on clay.

Walter Keeler who has made most types of kilns and fired with many different fuels says that *all* kiln firing relies heavily on the craftsman's skill and intuition. If firing by wood, for example, stoking must be controlled to take the pots, which may not be biscuited, through the critical stage from clay to pottery with reasonable economy of time and fuel. Experience will help you to read the signs of progress – the steamy blast of air through the spy bung, the colour change on the pots, the haze from the chimney, the look of the fire, the smell of the flames.

All kilns need patience as well as skill; in the end we put our pots into the fire and hope. Good luck potters!

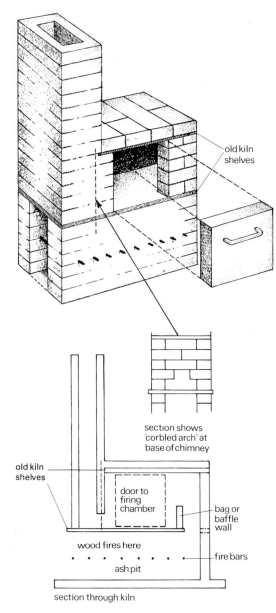

395(b) Wood-fired kiln, with door.

FURTHER WORK WITH GLAZE
by Lynne Reeve

Glaze defects and how to cure them

Having composed, applied and fired the glaze, along with the satisfactory results there will inevitably be some faulty glazes. Glaze defects cannot only spoil the appearance of a pot, they can even make it unusable. Some commonly occurring faults are crazing, edge chipping, pinholing and bubbling.

Crazing

Crazing is the name given to the network of fine cracks seen on some fired glazes. During the firing, both clay and glaze expand: as the pot cools, the clay and glaze contract, usually at different rates. If the contraction of the glaze is greater than that of the clay, the glaze will be put into a state of tension and will generally crack. Crazing in the glaze of a pot made of porous earthenware clay is a serious defect: the glaze will not provide a waterproof covering for the pot, which will therefore leak. In order to cure this defect it is usually sufficient to alter the composition of the glaze, though in rare cases of persistent crazing, the clay body itself may have to be adjusted. Since crazing is the result of too large a contraction on the part of the glaze, then the inclusion of materials which are known to contract very little on cooling can cure the problem. Such materials are referred to in text books as 'materials with low expansion coefficients', since if the expansion on heating is low, then the contraction on cooling will be correspondingly low.

For correct fit of glaze to clay, the glaze should have an expansion co-efficient which is lower than that of the clay. The following materials have been arranged in approximate order of size of expansion coefficient: the materials at the top of the list will tend to cause crazing and those near the end will help to eliminate it.

Some base glaze materials from Groups i, ii, iii and vi (see page 102), arranged in decreasing order of expansion coefficient:
(The expansion of colouring oxides (group iv) seldom influences the final fit of the glaze as we use them in such small quantities.)

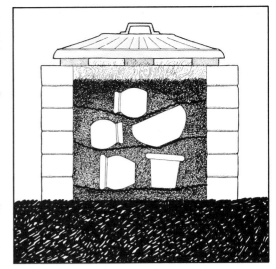

397 Section through a sawdust kiln using bricks, sawdust and chicken wire.

Nepheline syenite	(a feldspar-like material with a lower melting point)
Dolomite Soda feldspar Potash feldspar	(a stoneware flux/melting agent)
Whiting	(a flux/matting agent)
Barium carbonate Silica	(a flux/matting agent)
Magnesium carbonate	(a flux/matting agent)
Talc	(mainly a matting agent)
Zinc oxide	(an opacifier)
Spodumene, lepidolite and petalite	(feldspar-like materials with a higher melting point)
Lithium carbonate	(a low-temperature flux)

398 Raku equipment, asbestos gloves, tongs, sawdust, water, leaves.

If some of the 'highest expansion ingredient' in a crazed glaze is replaced by a low expansion material, crazing will be inhibited. It should be noted that the finer the craze pattern, the more serious the fault and the more difficult to correct; a large craze network signifies that very little alteration is necessary.

Delayed crazing
Sometimes a glaze which seems to fit a clay body perfectly after firing, may develop cracks months or even years later.

This phenomenon is known as delayed crazing. It is the result of the glaze expansion being insufficiently lower than that of the clay. The slight expansion of the body due to accumulated dampness over a period of time is enough to cause the glaze to craze.

Despite its obvious drawbacks, crazing can be used as a decorative feature; in fact the cracks in the glazes of some non-functional pots have sometimes been deliberately stained in order to emphasise the craze pattern (*399*). Examples of this can be seen on some Chinese Sung pots. This defect thus becomes a special effect called 'crackled glaze'.

99

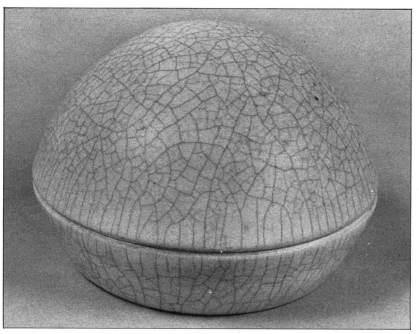

399 Small lidded porcelain box with crackle glaze enhanced by rubbed-in oxide stain, by David Leach.

400 Fluted dish, white Chingpai porcelain, China 12th-13th century. A superb example of a porcelain glaze.

Edge chipping and spiral cracking

Although these are not commonly occurring defects, they are an important feature of the glaze to clay 'fit' and are related to the more common 'crazing'. Edge chipping and spiral cracking occur when the expansion and hence contraction of the glaze is *considerably* lower than that of the body, not just sufficiently different to give a correct glaze fit, but so low as to cause a strong compressive force to be exerted on the clay; pieces of glaze can actually fall off the rim of the pot, an effect which is known as 'edge chipping'. The compressive force experienced by the body can even be sufficiently great to cause the pot to break in two. This break is most likely to occur at the weakest point, which in a thrown pot is along the line of a throwing ring. This is why the fault has become known as 'spiral cracking'. While crazing is a common fault, edge chipping or spiral cracking only occur if large quantities of materials of very low expansion, such as lithium carbonate or lithium compounds (lepidolite, spodumene and petalite), are used or if the clay has an unusually high coefficient of expansion.

Crawling

A crawled glaze is one which has run into thick masses or beads of glaze and left parts of the clay surface bare (401). This can occur if the glaze has been applied too thickly or it can be a result of dust or grease on the surface of the biscuited ware, which causes poor adhesion of glaze. It is possible for the glaze composition itself to be the reason for the crawling, if, for instance, there is too much clay included in the recipe. The shrinkage the glaze may experience on drying out and firing may result in areas of the clay body being exposed. The use of large quantities of magnesium carbonate and the opacifiers can also result in crawling.

Pinholing and bubbles

Pinholing is the name given to the tiny holes which sometimes appear on the surface of a fired glaze. These are tiny bubbles, which can often be the most difficult defect to eliminate as their cause is not always obvious. Here are some possible reasons and suggested cures:

(a) Rough particles on the clay surface may trap tiny pockets of air which remain after firing. The remedy for this fault is either to use a smoother clay or to coat the pot, when leather hard, in a smooth layer of clay slip. Alternatively, when the glaze has dried on the biscuited pot, the glaze can be gently rubbed, in an attempt to push the powder into the crevices, which might well be visible even before firing.

(b) There may be air bubbles in the liquid glaze often resulting from excessively vigorous stirring.

(c) The presence of too great a quantity of opacifier, which, though not large enough to cause crawling, is sufficient to cause pinholing.

(d) Certain materials, particularly manganese dioxide and barium carbonate, will sometimes cause bubbles, especially, though not exclusively, when they are used in large quantities. Their behaviour tends to be erratic; nine firings of a barium- or manganese-bearing glaze may be successful, but the tenth may produce a badly blistered surface.

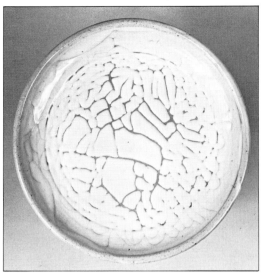
401 An example of 'crawling'.

Glaze calculation

In this chapter we have discussed empirical glaze making; for a potter interested in all aspects of glaze development, there are also more numerically based methods, which in principle allow qualities for a particular glaze to be arrived at by the use of a single process rather than by building up the glaze in cumulative stages. These alternative methods involve the calculation of glazes on a basis of molecular formulae and are explained in a number of ceramic text books including those listed in the Booklist.

Vapour Glazing

There is another method of glazing which is fundamentally different to that described so far, i.e. where a glaze in suspension is applied by hand to the biscuited pot. This alternative involves the use of fluxes which volatilise in a very hot atmosphere. This can be a highly dangerous process and expert knowledge is essential. The principle material used for this purpose is salt. Unglazed biscuited pots are packed into the kiln. (Salt firings are generally stoneware, earthenware salt firings are, for various reasons, far less common.) The kiln is fired almost to stoneware temperature, then damp salt is thrown in through the kiln firebox. The salt, which is a powerful flux, vapourises and combines with the alumina and silica of the clay body to form a glaze on the surface of the pots. Since the vapourised salt can fill every available crevice of the pottery, care must be taken to prevent the glaze sticking the pots to the shelf. The use of a highly refractory coating on the shelf, and small refractory pads of clay beneath the pot, or cunning undercutting of the pot base will overcome this problem. The type of clay used influences the colour and texture of the final salt glaze and the use of clay slips and colouring oxides can therefore help to give great variety to the salt glazed ware (*369, 371, 373, 402, 419*).

Salt glazing cannot be carried out in an electric kiln as the process would cause corrosion of the elements. *Also since a toxic vapour is produced, the firing should take place in an out-door kiln and local regulations should be respected.*

The first salt firing in a new kiln often produces rather meanly-glazed ware. This is because the salt is glazing the brickwork of the kiln as well as the pots. Once the kiln walls are well coated with salt glaze however, the firings will be more satisfactory. (A salt-glazed kiln will always affect other pots fired in it).

Salt glazing is the most commonly practised form of vapour glazing. However, a number of potters use washing soda instead of salt. The results are similar though highly erratic but no toxic fumes are produced.

402 Salt-glazed jar with beaten sides and round lid by Sarah Walton.

Suggestions for a series of glaze experiments

There are many valid approaches to empirical glaze making. The method outlined below is one which not only produces some pleasing and useful results, but also enables those who have had no previous experience of using glaze materials to build up a picture of the characteristics of the materials in a short space of time.
First, some of the most commonly used and readily available raw materials are listed below in six groups.

(i) Materials which contain all the ingredients needed in a glaze
i.e. silica, flux and alumina. These are arranged in order of decreasing fusibility. (The position of ash in the list is not significant, in that it covers a wide range of compositions.)

Lead frit, borax frit and calcium borate frit; nepheline syenite
soda feldspar; potash feldspar; lepidolite, spodumene and petalite
ash

A frit provides the basis for low temperature glazes; stoneware glazes can be based on one or more of the other materials. Detailed information on the composition of the frits is given in the suppliers' catalogues.

(ii) Fluxes
Whiting (which is powdered chalk, chemical name calcium carbonate)
Barium carbonate; dolomite (contains calcium and magnesium);
magnesium carbonate; talc (contains magnesium and silica);
wollastonite (contains calcium and silica)

(Talc and wollastonite cannot be considered as pure fluxes since they contain silica.)

(iii) Opacifiers
Tin oxide; zinc oxide; zirconium silicate; titanium oxide

(iv) Colouring oxides
Chromic oxide (grass greens); cobalt oxide or carbonate (blue)
Copper oxide or carbonate (greens and reds)
Iron oxide (blues, greens, browns, blacks)
Manganese oxide or carbonate (browns to purples)
Nickel oxide (greys and dull greens)
Rutile (impure titanium oxide) (tan and browns)
Vanadium pentoxide (yellows and dull browns)

(v) Clays
China clay; ball clay; red earthenware clay; local clay; bentonite

(vi) Sources of pure Silica
Flint; quartz

The experimental method

1 Select a material from list (*i*). Initially potash feldspar, soda feldspar, nepheline syenite or ash are the easiest to use; these materials provide a very good basis for the glaze, since they are almost glazes when fired alone.

2 Select any material from the fluxes in list (*ii*).

3 Use these two materials in a series of five tests which broadly cover the range of possible ratios of the two ingredients. For example, tests using potash feldspar and talc would be as follows:
Material A – potash feldspar (P.F.)
Material B – talc

Test number	Material A	Material B
1a	90%	10%
1b	70%	30%
1c	50%	50%
1d	30%	70%
1e	10%	90%

This range of tests provides a wide picture of the behaviour of talc and P.F. together. A 'finer' analysis can then be made over interesting ranges: if for example the results of test 1a and 1b are the most promising, a second set of tests can be made using smaller increases of talc, such as 85% P.F. + 15% talc and 95% P.F. + 5% talc.

If a number of different combinations of ingredients from list (*i*) and list (*ii*) are tried, and the data carefully recorded, valuable reference material will quickly be established and a number of useful glaze bases will emerge.

4 If a clay content is required in the glaze then some clay can be added to the simple glazes obtained from (3). Clay will make the glaze less shiny, so a base glaze must be selected with this in mind. If a clay content would otherwise spoil a particular glaze it should be remembered that bentonite is the clay which can be used in the smallest quantity.

5 These base glazes will already contain silica since it is present in all materials in list (*i*). However, some base glazes are improved by further silica additions (see list (*vi*)). Additions of 5%, 10% or 15% will usually be sufficient.

6 Having now obtained a base glaze, colour and opacity may be developed by the methods already outlined (using materials from (*iii*) and (*iv*) respectively).

Practical techniques in glaze testing

Quantity of test glaze:
40 grams dryweight will make sufficient wet glaze for several small test pieces. To avoid waste, small dishes and miniature sieves called 'cup sieves' can be used.

The test bowls:
A small bowl (approximately 2″ or 5 cm diameter) is generally accepted to be the best vehicle for a trial glaze, since it will display the finished glaze on both a concave and convex surface, and on a length of rim. The bowl shape will also contain a very fluid glaze and stop it running onto the kiln shelf.

Recording results

Glaze results must obviously be readily identifiable. Appropriate numbers or letters, written on the base of the test bowl in iron oxide, should be as simple and short as possible so that they are clearly legible after firing. Notes on the experiments are vital and it is worthwhile spending some time designing a reliable system of recording results. The glaze you use will have a profound effect on the finished pot. Since the glaze, its colour and texture, is as much an expression of the individual's intent as the actual form of the pot, many potters find the development of their own glazes and observation of the behaviour of the basic raw materials an essential part of their craft; you will be surprised how quickly you can build up your own range of interesting and beautiful glazes.

Lynne Reeve

Lynne Reeve became interested in ceramics seven years ago. She wanted to train as a thrower of functional domestic pots so joined the Studio Pottery course at Harrow School of Art. It was there that she first learned about glaze formulation and began her own programme of experiments.
Having completed the course, she then spent three years lecturing in Ceramic Chemistry at Harrow and other art colleges. In 1973 she went to Holland and worked in a small ceramics factory, throwing pots and developing glazes. She returned to England a year ago to complete her current project of glaze research at the Royal College of Art.

Pottery through the Ages

I have always believed that looking at examples of work from history gives a particular insight into how pots are made and eventually to that most elusive of goals 'the good pot'. The work we see now in museums and books reflects the aspirations of the potters from the past. Although they are quite rightly an expression of the age in which they were made they also, if they are good, have a timeless quality that speaks across the centuries. For me it helps to look at these pots and try to see the potter, the mark of the fingers perhaps, the way the various processes have been used, the type of mind behind the pot, humorous, austere, noble. The form, decoration, colour and texture will reveal a great deal about their maker and the age in which he worked. Some forms have a fullness about them that speak of confident times; colour can be bold and exuberant, or subtle and muted; the imagery used can tell of the peasant or the sophisticated aesthete. This chapter is only an appetiser, further reading and looking is necessary if you are to get the most from these beautiful and powerful objects from the past.

Saxon

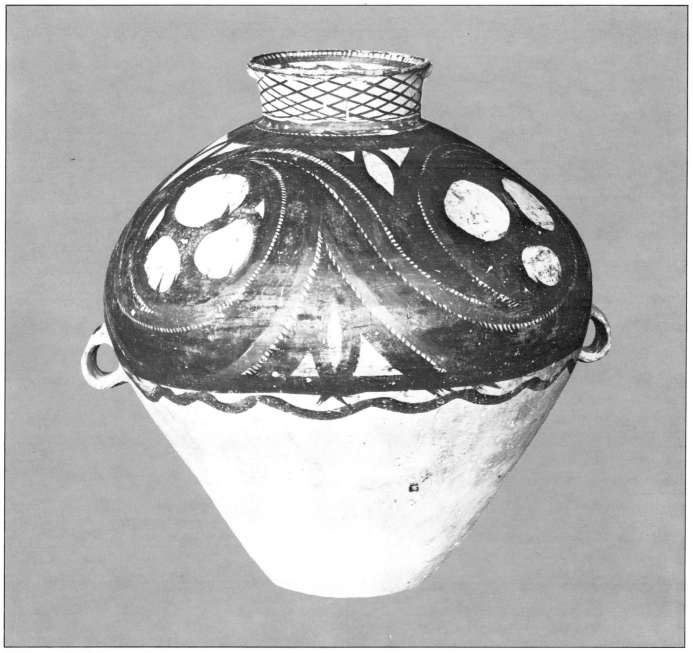

403 Neolithic coiled funerary jar, Kansu, China.

The earliest pots

Archaeologists are continually pushing back the dates of the first human artifacts and it now seems that pots have been made for about 10,000 years; the use of clay for modelling animals and human figurines is much older than that. For most of this time potters occupied the humbler levels of society, their work was utilitarian and expendable; some of the most lastingly beautiful work is of this kind. On some occasions however, pottery represented the highest achievement, technically and aesthetically, that men could reach. Minoan Crete, to give just one example, produced work in clay, pots and models, that was unsurpassed by other contemporary media (*349*). Indeed it is possible to study the history of pottery alongside other artistic traditions, but in the context of this book I have chosen to emphasise the technical demands and achievements which served the aesthetic vision of each age.

404 Pottery 'cakes' by Ernest Collyer.

Settled communities meant storage of surplus food, so from the time of the earliest Neolithic period, and in some cases even earlier, pots made from quite well-prepared clay were used for this purpose. They were handbuilt, usually coiled, and often reflected the forms of other materials like stone or basketry (*285*). This cross-reference with other materials is a feature that re-appears right the way through history to the present day when, although for different reasons, some potters imitate leather, metal or even jam tarts in clay (*404*). In older times the various materials often influenced each other, so that for example in early China we see bronze forms imitating clay forms but then later, clay pots bearing bronze features on them like ring handles that don't move. The Chevron pattern, obviously first derived from basket weave, is a universal decorative motif.

If we look back on our chart on decoration methods (page 54) we will find that these prehistoric pots used all the processes of decoration that take place before the first firing, especially incising, impressing and above all those employing the uses of slip. They were all low-fired, unglazed earthenware, whether they came from Neolithic China or Cyprus. The earliest were probably fired in kilns that were little more than bonfires, while others must have been fired in kilns having a fire-box and a separate area for the pots. The first method is still in use in places like Nigeria and Papua, the second you can find in present-day Crete for example. Certain types of pottery stand out from these earlier times; the coiled funerary urns from Kansu in north China, great rounded forms with strong swirling quite complex painting in slip (*403*); the tall majestic red clay shapes from pre-dynastic Egypt, their rims blackened from being stood upside down in the glowing ashes of the fire (*colour 20*); the delicately thrown slip-patterned bowls from Tel Halaf in Iran, and the strong forms with white inlaid decoration from early Cyprus (*303*). These and others like them from pre-historic and early historic times show that it is not a question of a steady climb towards perfection, there are simply peaks of achievement. These early potters using a simple technology made some of the strongest forms and most striking decoration ever produced.

405 Coiled 'spoon' form by Elizabeth Fritsch.

It is tempting once you leave the early period to see certain technical innovations such as the introduction of the wheel, the use of more finely 'levigated' clays (finer-particled), even higher firing temperatures, as evidence of a steady line of progress in pottery from early times, when so-called crude pots were made, to later and 'better' times. One can say that there is indeed a kind of 'urge to refinement' working all the way through the history of ceramics: the Attic vase of the 5th century BC is a summation of earlier Mediterranean types (*407*); the Chinese discovery of porcelain in the 9th century AD did set them and later Islam and Europe on a quest for whiteness, translucency and 'fineness'. But I believe that this would not represent a true picture of what has happened in pottery or of how all potters work. Even today there are potters who prefer to work with a more robust, earthy approach; compare a John Leach to a Mary Rogers pot (*back cover 2 and 3*). The history of pottery is really a kind of see-saw, embodying not only the rise and fall of different civilisations with their different techniques and demands on the potter, but also the ups and downs of changing attitudes and conditions within each age. For example in 12th century AD Sung dynasty China, exquisitely refined, jade-like porcelains were being made (*301*) alongside vigorous Tzu Chou stonewares and lead-glazed, low-fired earthenware (*1*). The ubiquitous 'chatti', the Mediterranean unglazed water-jar, was produced in its thousands at the same time as some Islamic potters were making delicately pierced bowls in fine white earthenware with transparent glazes that flowed over the holes to give a kind of tracery of tiny windows (*308*). Potters have always been of very varied types and have responded to widely differing demands. So it is worth remembering when looking, in museums and books, at pieces that in some cases represent the refined end of the spectrum of work made by potters, that along with these the humbler but no less good pots for everyday use were being made as well.

There are three main threads to the general history of pottery: the central one is the ceramic art of the Far East, especially China; the other two are Classical, then Christian Europe, and the Islamic world (which stretched at one time from Spain to the coast of China). Non-Islamic Africa and pre-Columbian America developed separately and do not begin to influence the West until our present century when their forms and decorations have had their effect on potters as different as Michael Cardew (*426*) and Elizabeth Fritsch (*405*). How all these threads intertwine and what forces of war and trade wove them together is a fascinating study.

406 Proto-Geometric bottle, thrown pieces joined together and turned, Cyprus 800 BC.

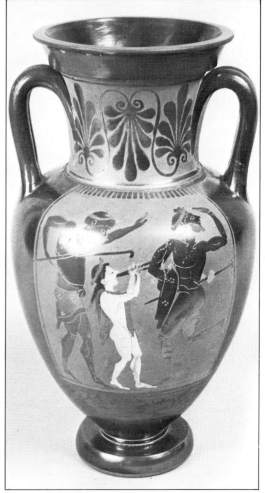

407 Attic amphora, 5th century BC, earthenware, thrown and turned joined pieces with figure painting decoration.

The classical world

Apart from the early Egyptian glazes (see glossary, *Egyptian paste*) and lead-glazed bricks from Assyria, the work from the Mediterranean world was essentially unglazed, slip-painted earthenware (porosity was not such a drawback in the hot climates). Early Greek ceramics, of the so-called archaic period, about 1000 BC (*2*), were lively, sometimes even amusing forms with decorations that had a limited earthy colour range but vivid imagery, whether of formalised lines and circles (*406*) or stylised animal and human figures. The Greek pots of the 5th century BC were technically the peak of this long era, that stretches from Crete of 2000 BC to Greece and then Rome of the 4th to 5th century AD, during which time the archetypal 'classical form' evolved – small base rising to a high belly that moved over rounded, sloping shoulders to a slender neck, symmetrical, smooth, the epitome of western perfection (*407*). The pots, made on the wheel, were often thrown in sections, joined and turned together to a perfect profile. Today Lucie Rie and Hans Coper (*408*) have both been affected, among other influences, by Classical forms and in this sense their work is essentially 'European' in marked contrast to Bernard Leach and his followers.

The painting on the Greek vases depended on a highly controlled use of finely levigated, cleverly blended slips and fluxes, with wonderful use of oxidising and reducing atmospheres in the kiln. This technology is at the heart of most classical decoration, whether in its formative stage as seen in proto-geometric Greek wares, or in the much later use the Romans

408 Group of oxidised stoneware forms by Hans Coper.

409 Modelled lady, buff coloured earthenware with traces of unfired pigment on white slip, T'ang dynasty China 618-906 AD.

made of potash and slip washes on their 'terra sigilata' (also called Arretine or Samian). By this time Roman potters, organised in factories, still made pots on the wheel but many were made by the mass production method of using clay in gypsum moulds. After the great age of unglazed slip the later Roman world began to use the lead glaze, probably taking it from the bordering empire of Parthia. By the 6th century AD the Christian-Roman Empire centred on Byzantium had developed lead-glazing further, spreading this technique, along with decoration that replaced Roman with Christian imagery, among the Middle Eastern and North African lands soon to become Islamic.

The Far East – China

China's history is as long and complex as that of Europe and her pottery has varied accordingly. If we think of a typical 'Classical' form as perfectly symmetrical, unglazed earthenware, then certainly a typical 'Chinese' form would be a more organic one, in richly glazed stoneware or porcelain. But like all generalised pictures this would be only partly true, especially of China, where the earlier glazed work was lead-glazed earthenware, and where plenty of unglazed pots were made in much later times. But the Chinese did make some stoneware probably as early as 1000 BC, and some with true feldspathic glazes as early as 200 BC, in early Han times. These latter, the Yüeh wares (*410*), were the forerunners of all the later celadons – a jade-like green glaze, the green coming from small quantities of reduced iron in the thick feldspar glazes. The Han

410 Yüeh pot from Han dynasty China, 206 BC-220 AD.

411 Lungchuan pot, 12th-13th century, Sung dynasty, China. Soft blue-green celadon glaze thrown pot with modelled clay decoration.

dynasty generally produced pottery forms that were based on metal-ware shapes; it was a time during which several foreign strains first began to come into China, Hellenistic decoration, for example and Buddhist teachings. But the scenes of domestic life, modelled figures and slab-built houses (*412*) are delightful evocations of this age when Confucianism was being codified, foreign policy was steadily expansionist, and life appeared to be ordered and rather sober. One potter to-day who has obviously derived inspiration from this kind of handbuilding is Ian Godfrey who often depicts houses with birds and animals reminiscent of this early Chinese work (*122*).

After the Han dynasty ended, the succeeding troubled times of the Six Dynasties period gave way to the brilliant flowering of the T'ang Dynasty (618-906 AD) when China seems to have burst into a rich cosmopolitan phase. Renewed contact with the West meant traders of many nationalities, purveyors of ideas, religious as well as stylistic, based on different techniques and materials. The pottery and modelling of the time reflect this outward-going, ebullient period. Brilliantly glazed fruit-like earthenware forms (*colour 16*), highly-coloured models of animal and human types – camels, horses, Armenians, Nestorian Christians – all were produced in great numbers (*118, 409*). The kilns must have been controlled to give a highly oxidising atmosphere when needed because the colours in their lead-glaze bases, such as honey-yellows from iron, browns from manganese, cobalt blues, copper greens and even antimony yellows were clear and even after many centuries still convey a sense of sparkle. The lead was probably imported from the fringes of the eastern Roman Empire. Alongside all these brilliant earthenwares the stonewares also developed during the T'ang period so that the aesthetic ideals and technical heights reached then set the standard for what was to follow. There was a profusion of pottery types, and towards the end of

412 Modelled 'sheep-pen' group in green glazed earthenware, from Han dynasty, China, 206 BC-220 AD.

the period, the ultimate outcome of the refined stonewares, came the invention of true white translucent porcelain. By the end of the T'ang and beginning of the next period, the Sung Dynasty, China could lay claim to being the supreme nation for high-fired ceramics. She has been, and these ancient pots continue to be the creative inspiration for most potters throughout the world.

T'ang

In the Sung Dynasty the exuberant earthenwares died down – politically it was a time of uncertainty, the ever-present menace of the nomadic invaders from the north-west gave a sense of foreboding – but all the main stoneware and porcelain types came to fruition. Painting and the other arts flowered under the patronage of an enlightened court and it was one of the rare moments in history when ceramics played an equal part with other creative activities. Pots were generally wheel-made, though throwing with added coil was often used to make the larger pieces. The modelling in clay and all the wheel forms too became gentler than in the previous era – a quiet haunting beauty so typical of Sung painting and poetry pervaded the work. The three Chinese modes of thought and belief, Taoism, Confucianism and Buddhism achieved a kind of synthesis.

In Sung times most of the decorative methods were used but the brushwork has surely never been equalled. The Emperors commissioned work especially for court use, huge numbers of pots were exported to all the Far Eastern countries, and we must never forget that the enormous production of everyday wares went on as a background to all this activity. No wonder someone has referred to China as a landscape with kilns!

Sung

The Chinese never clearly differentiated between stoneware and porcelain so that the term 'porcellanous stoneware' is used in historical accounts for what we would call the more refined kinds of stoneware. body. In Sung times, often as a result of the kind of body used, certain glaze types emerged:

1 The court celadons:
Ju – with a light green glaze.
Kuan – a similar celadon with a heavy crackle.
Lungchuan – with the most delicate blue-green glaze (*411*).
Ko – a darker-bodied equivalent of Lungchuan.

2 Northern Celadon – this has a dark, olive-green glaze, usually over elaborate carving and incising; it seems to have been made for more general use (*301*).

3 Chün – a kind of soft blue or blue-grey – it is still much sought after by today's stoneware potters (*colour 2*). The blue is a mysterious effect – not derived from cobalt or any physical blue but from the opalescent glaze trapping blue light.

4 Tzu Chou – altogether a more robust and peasant type using a buff body, often with a creamy slip glaze, and vigorous painting in black pigment (*1*).

5 Ching Pai – true porcelain with a white glaze – more appreciated now than in earlier times (*400*).

6 Chien – (tenmoku in Japanese) the dark lustrous brown-black iron glaze that can resemble oil spots or hare's fur and break to orange when on thin edges. It is also much beloved by studio potters in the West, for example, David Leach and Ray Finch. I myself use this luscious iron glaze on my big jugs, and in fact many potters have their own tenmoku (*colour 7 and 12*).

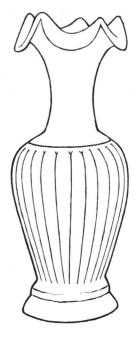

T'ang

413 Red stoneware teapot. Yi-hsing, China, 17th Century.

Eventually in the 13th Century the nomads overran China, the Islamic Yuan dynasty succeeded the Sung and the greatest age of ceramics closed. But many fine examples of the potter's art were still to come from China: Blue and White porcelain – 'Ching-te-chen' (*back cover 5*) – with its painting in cobalt oxide, the exquisite Ming porcelains, some of them austere with copper-red brush strokes, others with over-glaze enamels on complicated, highly ornate decorations. Porcelain factories producing at times enormous vases, thrown, coiled and turned, tended to oust the older, more localised centres of stoneware, but these never died out and in a later phase the interesting 'Yi Hsing' unglazed tiny red stoneware teapots (*413*) and jars were exported to Europe with the tea where they had a great effect on the potters there.

The qualities of refinement typified by the pottery of China, particularly of these later dynasties, continued to influence the Western potters for a long time to come; the various Courts of the Kings and Princes of Europe vied with each other as they strove to emulate the Eastern examples.

The Far East – South East Asia and Korea

If China dominated the Far East, other countries there were also making fine ceramics in styles derived from technical innovations of their own. South East Asia was renowned for fruit-like forms, with beautifully liquid-looking celadon glazes, coming from Thailand and Vietnam. Korea had 3 main dynasties: Silla, Koryo and Yi. The Koryo dynasty approximated in time to Sung China and was greatly indebted to her for techniques and aesthetics; nevertheless it produced some uniquely serene work: pots, clay-modelled figures and pots with modelled additions – knobs, handles, animal decorations, etc. The inlaid clay technique later called by the general name of 'Mishima' seems to have been a Korean invention (*colour 9*). The Yi dynasty, mainly a time of harsh poverty, gave to the world some of the most rugged forms and strongest brush decoration – flowers, flying birds and fish (*colour 10*).

Although Bernard Leach was introduced to pottery in Japan and became a recognised master in that country, it was to Chinese Sung dynasty wares and to the Koryo and Yi dynasties of Korea that he has constantly turned throughout his life. He and his many followers have helped spread the appreciation of the qualities that Chinese and Korean pots share.

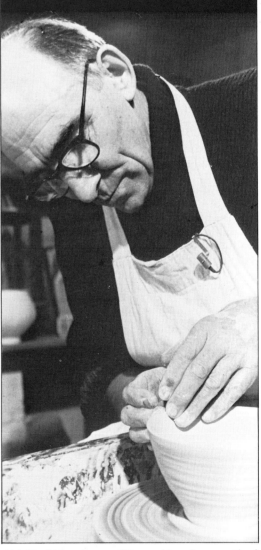

414 David Leach, son of Bernard Leach, apprenticed to his father and worked alongside him as student, manager and partner until he set up his own workshop in Devon. Today he is one of Britain's leading potters, making stoneware and porcelain of both a domestic and individual character, which is exhibited all over the world.

Qualities of rightness of materials, decoration that blends harmoniously with the forms, work that has a quiet strength that makes it seem more a part of nature than of man. Today David Leach's work aspires to these qualities, in his use of porcelain and his subtle decoration (*370, 399, 414, back cover 1*).

The Far East – Japan

In Neolithic times the off-shore islands of Japan produced some most original handbuilt pots. These 'Jomon' pots were coiled and beaten, often with cord-marked impressions on their surfaces (the word means 'cord-beaten'), and incorporated elaborate added and carved clay decoration, usually towards the tops of their forms (*318*). Almost from the start one supreme quality of Japanese work stands out, that of asymmetrical balance. It is said that Japan is a country of earthquakes and mountains – there are few flat or level features; impermanence, sudden change even surprise might seem built into their way of life; this is reflected in their ceramics. There is certainly a love of roughness, naturalness that runs through much of the Japanese aesthetic and selects the 'fault' – the split in a pot wall, the crawl of thick glaze – as having a natural unsophisticated beauty worthy of notice. It is equally true that a meticulous, delicate beauty, epitomised by the exquisitely carried out miniature brush marks on some Japanese paper-thin porcelain shows another side of their appreciation of the arts.

Korean

415 Raku, black glazed tea bowl by Koetsu, Japan 1588-1637.

For many centuries after the end of the Jomon period Japan was under the sway of China. 'Yayoi' wheel-made forms were strong and interesting, while the 'Haniwa' tomb figures (*416*) – a combination of thrown, slab-built, coiled and modelled techniques were spectacularly so. But it was not until the end of the Sung period, when Japan was compelled to keep out the Mongol (Yuan) invaders that she began to gain a ceramic tradition all her own. The tea ceremony headed by Zen Buddhist tea-masters was at the centre of the arts and manners of the time. The kilns involved in making the water pots, the Raku drinking vessels (*415*) and the tea containers for this aid to Zen meditation were to

416 'Haniwa' tomb figure Japan.

417 Water jar from Bizen, Japan 17th century.

Persian

become famous by the 17th century. The types of ware made are usually named by the district from which they come: they include the powerful pots from *Tamba*; subtle straw-burnt *Bizen* pots coloured brown to orangey-red by their long fire (*417*); *Iga* ware water-pots famous for their battered, even split, walls; coarse-grained pots of *Shigaraki*. Japanese pottery and particularly the Zen spirit of the immediate, exercises one of the most powerful influences in modern ceramics; Australia, America as well as Britain feel its force. No one potter epitomises this spirit more than Hamada, the world-famous Japanese potter (*125*, *colour 1*), who has worked at Mashiko near Tokyo since 1923. Some of the old kilns are still in use today so that in Japan tradition has never been broken as it was by the Industrial Revolution in England. There is a huge modern Japanese ceramic industry, but the old hand methods have never died out. The master potters have become classified by the Government as 'Living National Treasures', their work coveted by collectors all over the world.

The Middle East

The long and varied history of this area, stretching at one time from the bounds of Europe in the north west to Asia proper in the east, in ceramic terms seems to have a common base in Classical forms. Where the Greek and Roman world left its impression it lasted, so that Hellenistic forms, for example, often seem to intermingle with succeeding decorative styles, late Byzantine and Sassanian motifs giving way later to the dominant Islamic in the 7th or 8th century AD. Technically wheel-made pots dominated, but the production of tiles for decorating mosques became a major industry (*104*). Most pots were unglazed humble waterpots and simple cooking vessels, but the sandy body did lend itself to both lead and alkaline glazing, firing at relatively low earthenware temperatures; and it was in this area that the major aesthetic developments took place.

418 Persian ewer, Islamic calligraphy under a turquoise glaze, 13th century.

From the late 8th century onwards traders from the caravan routes across Central Asia brought examples first of stoneware, then later of porcelain from China (a major battle fought between Arab and T'ang armies brought many Chinese prisoners into the Islamic countries of eastern Persia – some of them were potters). Once the desirability of true porcelain was felt the search began for the formulae that would lead to more refined results. Attempts were made by Middle Eastern Potters to simulate fine white porcelain, but their natural resources, the right kind of clays and minerals as well as their inability to reach sufficiently high temperatures were always against them. (In fact true porcelain was not made even in the West until the beginning of the 18th century in Germany.) Ashes of tin were mixed with the glazes used to try and achieve one attribute of porcelain – whiteness. This led to painting on top of the opaque glaze (maiolica) eventually in a polychrome palette – copper, manganese, iron and cobalt – in oxidising kilns. Eventually bodies were refined, white slip coatings applied, temperatures raised and even glass mixed in to the clay to attempt an approximation of the other two characteristics of porcelain, hardness and translucency.

But if the ultimate goal of porcelain escaped the potters of the Islamic Middle East there were other achievements to compensate. Their sense of spatial relationships over the surfaces of their painted pottery, especially when they used the two styles of writing, Kufic and Naski, was masterly (*418*). When they added to this ability the technique of reduced earthenware lustres they produced a completely unique contribution to the art of the potter (*364*). Using precious and semi-precious metals, gold, silver and copper they had at their command a range of silvery yellows and rich ruby-red colours in which to paint their rhythmic imagery, both abstract and, in spite of the much-quoted embargo on figure work, human and animal forms. Persian lustrewares are some of the abiding joys from ceramic history and 'Hispano-Moresque' lustre plates, made during the Moorish occupation of Spain, are among the most powerful painted images created by potters (*colour 13*). Few potters today continue the technique but among them, Alan Caiger-Smith's work stands out (*colour 11*).

European

One other decorative process can also be attributed to the Islamic potters: enamel painting on top of the fired glaze. Persian 'Minai' wares, mainly deep bowls showing richly caparisoned horses and camels with their riders, probably derive from the miniature illuminated manuscripts painted for the Persian Court (*colour 14*). All three of these particularly Islamic innovations were taken over by the European potters, tin-glaze Maiolica, lustreware and eventually via China, enamel painting. The latter influenced the Chinese from the Yuan dynasty onwards until like all 'foreign' influences it was absorbed into the Far Eastern tradition. That lightness of touch, sense of bright but subtle colour so characteristic of the best of Islamic Middle Eastern work is seen on the lustreware Egyptian dish (*364*), and see how the modelling of the bird's head has been used to decorative effect (*colour 6*). They were, above all else, brilliant decorators.

Europe

In pottery terms the final legacy of Rome to Europe was lead-glazed earthenware with slip decoration, either painted, sgraffito or trailed (*345*). Besides the humbler, unglazed household pots they were the only types found until about 1000 AD. After this the Islamic techniques of tin-glazed Maiolica ware and lustre-decorated ware gradually became more common in Southern Europe. The lustre-ware centres were chiefly in Spain (where the Moors long held sway over Christian subjects and produced a combination of Islamic technique and Christian imagery)

Maiolica

and Italy. With the Renaissance the Italian centres of Deruta and Gubbio evolved distinctive styles (*colour 4*). Maiolica has had a longer and wider history; tin-glazed ware goes under many names: Maiolica (*colour 3*) (the name is said to have come from Majorca, island centre for Arab traders), Faience (from Faenza) and Delft (hence Dutch Delft, Bristol and Lambeth Delft). Until the harder 17th century saltglaze stonewares, and refined 18th century Wedgwood earthenwares it was probably Europe's most widely used pottery. It is still made today in some European centres and of course by some individual artists, potters like Alan Caiger-Smith. It has always had, however, a southern Mediterranean or Islamic flavour which serves to highlight the difference between northern and southern Europe. Northern Europe tended towards a sparer, simpler style, the south towards greater flamboyance. German saltglaze stoneware developed from the 15th century onwards and was exported for the wine trade all over the northern part of the continent – England receiving its fair share through its eastern ports. The 'Bellarmine' bottle with its sprigged greybeard decoration is a good example of this type of ware (*419*). Saltglaze, enjoying something of a revival among young studio potters today, by its very nature can be somewhat hard and austere; much of it is earthy in colour, in marked contrast to the tin-glazed earthenware. Moreover, the lead-glazed peasant wares stemming from the older Romano-British or Gaulish traditions, jugs and cooking pots from Britain, northern France and the Low Countries had become part of everyday life by the early Middle

419 German salt-glaze stoneware Bellarmine bottle, 16th century.

420 Medieval jug, slip-trailed dots and lines.

Ages (*191, 420*). They were low fired, robust shapes greatly admired by some present day potters. Some of these pots had slip decoration usually only coloured by iron or perhaps copper, over which the powdered raw lead (galena) was sprinkled to make the glaze. So the whole feel of pottery from the north, whether salt-glaze or lead-glaze, was different from its southern counterpart. Anyone today looking at a Medieval British jug will see immediately that the form and decoration belong to a different world from a Maiolica or lustre jug of the same date from Italy or Spain. This difference persisted when the medieval wares developed into the slip-wares of Britain and Northern Europe. Slip-trailed 17th and 18th century wares were prevalent over a very wide area (*347*) and in Britain every village had its own potter serving the demand of its small community. A few potters, such as Peter Dick, are still using the slip-trailing technique today (*346*); Mary Wondrausch made the *'Craft of the Potter'* title plates by this method (*421*). But the forces of change were gathering in the form of rising populations, the higher living standards of a rising middle class and the development of several technical 'improvements' in ceramics that enabled more refined products to meet a growing market for standardised wares. The Industrial Revolution saw the rapid growth of urban centres, some of them devoted to specific industries, such as the Staffordshire area centred around Stoke-on-Trent for pottery. Josiah Wedgwood is said to have 'found a craft and left an industry', and it is certainly true that by the time of his death about 1800 a very great change was coming about in the whole business of making pottery. Machines were doing an increasing amount of the work, and what hand-work remained was split into even more divisions; the assembly-line machine age was in sight. Mass production methods, casting, easily reproducible decorative means like transfer prints, standardised bodies and glazes accounted for the overwhelming number of pots made. Factories making ceramics to an extremely high standard of finish and function grew up in most European countries, often on the sites of earlier pottery centres; these ceramics were even, in some cases, beautiful examples of industrial design.

The village potter with his slip-decorated lead-glazed ware took over a hundred years to disappear but his demise began in the mid 18th century with the beginning of modern times.

Today the world is divided into industrialised and relatively non-industrialised nations. Some indigenous pottery still remains in these latter places but even there it is either fast disappearing or being debased by tourist demands. It is inconceivable that this process of industrialisation will be reversed, but the more machines are designed to make the vast majority of the ceramic objects we need, the more people will want to experience at first hand the uses of clay as an expressive material — and will want the work of individual, artist potters.

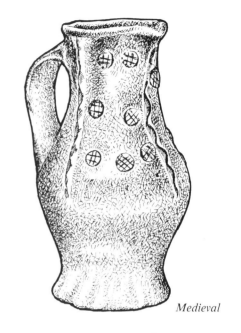
Medieval

421 Slip-trailed earthenware dish by Mary Wondrausch.

Pre-Columbian pottery

Pre-Columbian pottery is a completely separate strand in the history of pottery and developed independently from the others.

The potters from Central and Southern pre-European America recorded, with their models and their paintings on pots, detailed information as to the everyday lives, domestic, religious, even sexual, led by their extraordinary civilisation. Luckily the 16th century conquistadors who in the end destroyed this way of life sent back to Europe ceramics as well as gold and silver, and recent archaeology has discovered much more since then. The earliest pottery found so far dates back to about 3200 BC, but the great age of ceramics coincided with the climax of their civilisation and lasted for a thousand years up to 1000 AD. The pre-Columbian craftsmen were noted for their gold and silver work and their

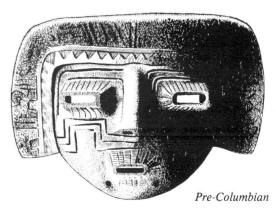
Pre-Columbian

weaving, but it was clay that they used most widely. Domestic vessels, spinning- and loom-weights, musical instruments from rattles to trumpets, building bricks and tiles, religious models of gods, ritual vessels for sacred rites and burial pots were all made in countless numbers over this huge area that stretched from what is now southern Mexico down through Central America to the west coast and southern Peru and Chile. Certain types of pottery, like stirrup shapes (*back cover 4*), the high-legged bowls and pots are unique, and the complexity of some of their ornate designs has no parallel.

The wheel, except, strangely, on childrens toys, was never used so all ceramics were handbuilt. Three main methods were used, often in combination: hand-modelling, press-moulding into and over fired clay moulds (*423*), and coiling. The surfaces were smoothed to take the elaborate painting in pigments, which were mostly the usual mineral oxides, although colours of organic vegetable origin were used as well. As many as eight colours were used by potters, so that when we conjure up a picture of this work it is one of bright if earthy colours, burnished sometimes to a high polish, on forms that have a feeling very different from most ceramics from the rest of the world. It is difficult to pin down but it has something to do with the freedom of these handbuilt forms.

Among so much splendid work it is difficult to choose, but some examples stand out even if only to highlight the great range of forms and treatments used by this fantastic civilization. The polychrome painted work from the Nazca region of southern Peru, with its lively and very mixed imagery of monsters and human heads, beautifully placed on the extremely well-made pots, is probably the finest painting produced in South America (*424*). Further to the north the Mochica potters made an amazing array of shapes, stirrup-pots, animal and human forms, often in a close range of creams and browns, some burnished, with the finest modelling imaginable (*422*). If you add to this the subtle low-relief carving on the Mayan pots from Central America (*425*), you can grasp something of the range these pre-Columbian potters achieved.

The clay, especially in the more advanced times, was extremely well prepared, tempered with a variety of ingredients, crushed rock, ash, sand, mica that glittered like gold, and powdered shells. Both oxidising and reducing atmospheres were used to control colours, and although no true glaze was used a few centres made a kind of lead-based vitrified slip as an inlay or covering over some wares. The kilns used never seem to have reached more than low earthenware temperatures, about 900°C.

It is above all to the astonishing imagery of these handbuilt forms that the contemporary potter turns. Here the sense of pattern, whether shown by a row of gruesome captive warrior heads, or more pleasantly by repeated and interlocking bird forms, is most powerful. Potters like Helen Pincombe (*58*) and later Elizabeth Fritsch, both using the coiling technique, have been influenced by it and Elizabeth Fritsch, though not burnishing the surface of her pots, does use pigment loaded with different coloured oxides to paint on her geometric designs in a highly personal and contemporary manner (*colour 15*).

Africa

All non-industrial pottery coming from a tribal society, whether from Africa, Papua or the Xingu Indians of the Amazonian jungle, have one thing in common – a marvellous treatment of handbuilt raw clay, both in form and decoration.

The huge African continent provides many examples to confirm this statement (*428*). The wheel is used only by Islamic Potters (mainly in the

422 Mochica parrot stirrup-pot, cream and brown burnished clay.

Pre-Columbian

African

423 Pre-Columbian pot, press-moulded and modelled clay form, earthenware, 8th century AD.

424 Coiled earthenware pot with painted faces, Nazca, pre-Columbian Peru, 7th century AD.

425 Earthenware bowl with carved decoration, Mayan, pre-Columbian central America.

north) where it is the men who are more usually employed in making pots. Over most of the rest of the country pot-making is women's work, closely connected with the other functions of her domestic life. The methods used are, in the main, coiling, pulling or stroking up from a lump of clay and adding coils at a later stage (Ladi Kwali uses this technique (427)), or placing one very thick coil upon another and then squeezing and beating them together and then into shapes. The forms themselves have round or conical bases as befits a village environment where walking to the well, pot on head, is a daily occurrence and where floors are of soft earth or sandy soil. They have a wonderful feel of internal volume which comes both from their traditional function and the way they are slowly and rhythmically beaten into shape. In this century Western artists, painters and potters, were among the first to realise the tremendous power of these pots, the force of which comes not only from the full forms of the water, beer and cooking pots but from the incised, burnished and added clay decoration. Sticks, shells, roulettes often of metal are used to make these unglazed marks and burnishing, sometimes greatly enhanced by adding graphite to the area, is skilfully done with smooth pebbles or metal objects. The colour range is earthy, from greys to blacks, and all the unglazed iron colours from pinky-buff to deep red. White slip-painted inlay often relieves other clay colours.

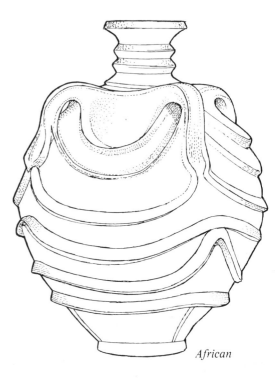

African

427 Pinched and coiled pot with incised decoration by Ladi Kwali; see also 51, 52.

426 Stoneware bottle by Bawa Ushafa from Michael Cardew's workshop in Abuja.

428 Nigerian ceremonial pot with added clay birds as decoration – low-fired earthenware.

The preparation of the clays and 'tempering' materials, usually crushed shells or grog from pounded-up fired pots, is so well understood as decreed by traditional methods that the amazing bonfire kilns can fire the pots, sometimes very large indeed, in a matter of one or two hours, and in many cases far less. Many African potters pre-heat their pots over a low fire, but usually they are simply heaped up in a seemingly haphazard way and covered with brushwood, which when set alight burns fiercely, firing the pots to temperatures not much higher than 900°C. Some are 'waterproofed' with mixtures of vegetable matter as they emerge from the fire, others receive treatment before the firing begins. In either case decoration is enhanced by this process. The whole procedure of making, decorating and firing such African pots is a natural part of the near-subsistence level of these potters' lives.

Indeed clay plays a vital role for those Africans still living in tribal societies. They use it not only for pots, and their many models of humans and animals, but for drums and other musical instruments. In some areas their houses, resembling huge handbuilt pots, are made of it. They employ a simple technology but it produces these magnificent forms with their striking decoration. The work will remain a testimony to a way of life that is probably coming to an end. Many of the later pots made by Michael Cardew (*426*), who spent 25 years working with Nigerian potters, owe their forms to African influence. His great book, *Pioneer Pottery*, based on his lifetime's work, includes his experiences in Western Africa.

The Western revival

The Victorian age, served by a highly competent technology, developed such embellishments to both form and decoration that it had by the latter part of the century lost sight of the natural material, clay. The inevitable reaction was headed by thinkers like Ruskin and Morris; potters such as William De Morgan and later the Martin brothers began to make pots by hand again, and it seems that in other parts of the world too, a few people were seeking to get back to fundamentals.

In the late 20's in Germany this feeling culminated in the Bauhaus, a school that sought a return to the understanding of basic materials and design principles. In Britain it is to those potters who were young in the early part of this century that we owe the revival of interest in pots and clay as an expressive medium. Bernard Leach and William Staite Murray (*429*), in their different ways affected the course of events more than anyone else. Murray believed that pottery was a Fine Art form worthy to stand beside any other on equal terms; his many students, most of whom went into the Colleges of Art, have taught the same message. Bernard Leach, whilst not denying this, has always, through his work and his many books, added the belief in clay as a natural material for making pots for use. He looked to the anonymous peasant potters of the past for his spiritual influence. He has tried to marry the spirit of Eastern pottery with that of pre-industrial England. He stresses the use of natural, unrefined materials and hand processes with the acceptance of the somewhat fortuitous effects that come from this direct, first-hand experience with clay and fire. He returned from Japan in 1920 and wrote his major work *A Potter's Book* in 1939. It still remains the potter's Bible. After the second World War a whole new generation of young potters, some in the workshops inspired by Leach, started making functional pots for use in the home, as a kind of antidote to industrially-made production; others in the Art Colleges studied ceramics as an art form. Since then the potters in Britain have grown in number and range until now there is hardly a country that has such a wealth of people

429 Large stoneware bottle, tenmoku glaze and iron painting by William Staite Murray, late 1930's.

enjoying making pottery – as amateurs, teachers or professionals – and others like myself who would see themselves as a mixture of all three!

Today potters have the whole history of ceramics to look to for inspiration. It is sometimes a bewildering experience: I believe that we can be helped to an understanding by looking at the way clay was used to make pots in the past; we should also remember that the decorations the potters used had special meanings for them in their own time.

We too surely should strive to discover the ways of making and the imagery that together express ourselves and our own age.

430 Oxidised stoneware by Hans Coper, 3 wheel-made forms joined together.

431 Large lead-glazed slipware bowl by Michael Cardew.

century	Middle East	Far East	
		China	Japan
AD			
20			
19			
18		Yi-Hsing red stoneware	
17	Isnik Turkish painted ware		Tea masters Raku
16		*Ming* porcelain: blue and white painting at best	Beginnings of Tea ceremony
15			
14	Minai enamels	*Yuan* (Islamic) dynasty blue and white fine stoneware and porcelain	Distinctly Japanese style
13	Best period for lustres		
12	Oxide painting		
11	on lead glaze	*Sung* – celadon Chien Chun Tzu Chou	
10	and tin glaze		
9		T'ang first porcelain Horses, figures, pots	
8	*Islamic period* begins	*T'ang* dynasty bright earthenware glazes	
7			
6	*Sassanian* influence	Stonewares continue	Chinese influence
5			First stoneware
4	*Byzantine* influence	*6 Dynasties* Stonewares develop	Haniwa – tomb figures
3	Lead glazing spreads		Throwing begins
2			Yayoi ware
1	Roman influence Hellenistic Greek	First feldspar-glazed stoneware Yüeh	
BC		*Han* dynasty Lead glazing	
500	Lead glazing Mainly unglazed earthenware	Ashglazed pots *Chou* dynasty	
1000	*Assyrian* lead-glazed tiles	First unglazed stoneware *Shang* dynasty	Jomon
2000	Egyptian paste	Neolithic period	handbuilt
3000	Throwing begins Pre-dynastic Egypt	Kansu	pots
4000			
5000			

Middle East: EARTHENWARE – THROUGHOUT WHOLE PERIOD

China: EARTHENWARE · STONEWARE · FULLY GLAZED STONEWARE · PORCELAIN

Japan: EARTHENWARE · STONEWARE · PORCELAIN

	Europe	Pre-Columbian America	century
Korea			AD
			20
			19
	European porcelain		18
	Slipware		
Yi dynasty	Country		17
	potter		
robust shapes	tradition		16
	Stoneware	European	15
strong painted	German saltglaze	conquest	
	Hispano-Moresque lustres	*Inca*	14
decoration			
	Renaissance Italian		13
	Maiolica		
elegant stoneware	Medieval		12
and porcelain	British jugs		
Mishima inlay		*Chimu*	11
			10
Koryo dynasty			
			9
			8
			7
	Saxon food vessels		6
	mostly unglazed		
		Classical period	5
		Maya	4
		Nazca	3
Silla dynasty		*Mochica*	2
unglazed food vessels			1
	Roman terra-sigilata		
	Hellenistic period	All hand-built	BC
	Lead glazing begins		
Pre-*Silla*	Greek Attic figure-		500
	painting		
	Archaic Greek		1000
	Cretan Amphora		2000
	octopus painting		AD
		3500BC	3000
		discovery of first pots	4000
			5000

PORCELAIN — STONEWARE — EARTHENWARE

PORCELAIN — STONEWARE — LEAD GLAZED EARTHENWARE — EARTHENWARE

LEAD GLAZED EARTHENWARE EUROPEAN TRADITION

LOW FIRED EARTHENWARE THROUGHOUT WHOLE PERIOD

Glossary

Ash glaze A glaze made with varying proportions of wood or vegetation-derived ash, sometimes together with clays, feldspars and other minerals. Different ashes impart their own distinctive colours and textures to glazes.

Ball clay A plastic secondary clay, stands high temperature and fires off-white.

Biscuit or bisque Ware which is fired to a state hard enough to facilitate handling in glazing. In many cases it also makes some decorative techniques simpler to achieve.

Body The substance from which the work is finally made; rarely just a clay, usually a balanced blend of clays, feldspars, quartz (silica) and other non-plastic 'opening' ingredients like sand or grog which together form a satisfactory combination for working and firing.

Bone china An English form of porcelain originally made to compete with Oriental true hard-paste porcelain. The body consists of 40-50% calcined ox bones, which lowers the vitrification point and produces whiteness and translucency.

Borax A powerful flux in many glazes and frits; calcined borax, not ordinary borax is usually used because of its high water content.

Burnishing Compacting the surface of a pot or slip coating on a pot to give a polished finish. Hard smooth objects like pebbles or spoons are used.

Calcine To heat to red heat or more, after which the material is usually crushed ready for use.

Calcium Carbonate Whiting, chalk, limestone and some marbles. All make approximately the same kind of middle- and high-temperature fluxes.

Cast To make shapes by pouring liquid clay (slip) into moulds usually made from plaster of Paris.

Celadon A name given to a whole range of stoneware and porcelain glazes ranging in colour from light grey-green to deep olive-green, produced by small amounts of iron in a reduction atmosphere.

Chün A thick high-fired opalescent glaze first made by the Chinese; beautiful light blues can be obtained without the use of cobalt, but when reduced iron is present in small amounts.

Coiling To form pottery by the use of rolls of clay welded together.

Cone Small conical object made of compressed graduated glaze materials with a known melting point, used to indicate the temperature reached in a kiln at a given point.

Crackle A more or less controlled crazing of glaze for decorative effect: oxides are sometimes rubbed in to enhance the pattern.

Crawling When the fired glaze retracts to expose the bare body.

Crazing The cracking of the glaze in fine lines caused by uneven tension between glaze and body during cooling. The process is sometimes long delayed. It is considered a defect in earthenwares because they are porous and the vessel will not then hold liquid.

Delft Dutch and English earthenware, coated with a lead glaze opacified with tin oxide. Metal oxides are painted on the glaze before firing to give the characteristic colours, such as blue (cobalt), green (copper), browny-mauve (manganese) and yellow (antimoniate of lead). Also known as maiolica and faience, it first made its appearance in the Middle East.

Dunting The breaking or cracking of pots while cooling after firing – caused by cold air getting into the kiln.

Earthenware One of the three main types of pottery, the others being stoneware and porcelain. It is opaque, relatively soft, and porous unless covered with an uncrazed glaze. The firing temperature can be as low as 800°C, as with some African pottery, or as high as 1200°C before it starts to vitrify, and technically becomes stoneware.

Egyptian Paste A body first used in ancient Egypt to make jewellery and small models. The soluble fluxing ingredient, soda, was mixed in with the other substances (mainly quartz and copper carbonate) so that it migrated outwards as the water evaporated leaving a glazed surface. The copper carbonate gave the typical Egyptian turquoise green but other carbonates such as manganese and cobalt can be used for other brilliant colours. The work is fired to about 950°C.

Enamels Low-temperature coloured glazes used on top of already fired high-temperature glazes.

Engobe Another word for a slip, often used for slip coatings on coarse bodies and slips especially compounded for use on biscuited bodies.

Eutectic The lowest melting point of two or more substances.

Faience French earthenware. See Delft.

Feathering A method of decorating by drawing the tip of a feather across lines of wet slip to give a characteristic pattern.

Fettle To finish the surface of leather-hard or dry clay by removing unwanted marks, especially seams made by casting moulds.

Flux Any substance that lowers the melting point of a ceramic body, glaze or colour. Glazes are usually named after the chief flux used in a particular mixture, eg: dolomite glaze, talc glaze, etc.

Frit A material used in glazes and on-glaze enamels usually on low-temperature ware. Frits are made by heating, shattering and grinding certain substances together whereby soluble or toxic substances can be made safely usable.

Fusibility The ability to melt; a fusible glaze would be one that melted to a smooth glassy finish or surface.

Galena Lead sulphide used as a glaze, for example on English medieval earthenware pots.

Gilding Overglaze gilding is fired on to an already-fired glaze surface at about 800°C. Flux, gold in various forms, a little gum arabic, are mixed together – after the firing the gold may have to be burnished; silver can also be used in this way.

Glaze An impervious vitreous coating on pottery, usually produced by the fusion of silica with alumina by means of a flux. It can range in both visual and tactile quality from a dull, rough, matt surface to a very smooth and shiny one.

Greenware Unfired pottery.

Grog Fired, crushed and ground clay added to modify a clay body. You can buy grog in certain mesh sizes such as 30 to 60 for handbuilding or 60 to dust for finer work.

Gum arabic and tragacanth Natural gums mixed in to help glazes and oxides to stay on the pot while it dries and then fires.

Handbuilding To make pots or other forms by any method other than throwing on a wheel or mechanical process; usually refers to pinching, coiling and slabbing techniques.

Jiggering and Jolleying A mechanical method of making repetition shapes, usually simple shapes such as plates and cups on the wheel with plaster moulds and profiles.

Leather-hard Clay when it is stiff but still damp enough to be joined to other pieces with slip, or have handles, lugs, knobs, etc., joined to it; also called cheese-hard.

Levigation Method of refining clay by floatation in water: allowing the heavier particles to settle and the smaller particles to be taken off, the process being repeated until the finest particles are separated out.

Lustre A film-like coating of metal or metallic oxide applied to the already-fired glazed surface, and fused onto it in a second firing at the low temperature of 600-800°C.

Lute To join leather-hard clay surfaces together, with slip or slurry.

Maturing temperature The point at which a clay can be said to have fired to its correct strength or a glaze to have properly fused or melted.

Oxidation Firing a kiln with an oxidising atmosphere, one which has an adequate supply of air, to enable metals in clays and glazes to give their oxide colours, greens from copper and honey colours from iron. Electric kilns give oxidising firing unless a reducing agent is introduced. See *Reduction*.

Porcelain True oriental porcelain, also known as hard-paste, contains china clay, feldspar and silica; it is fired at about 1300°C or higher, is translucent when thin, usually white and extremely hard. In the West, various bodies eg soft-paste porcelain and bone china, were made in imitation of true porcelain.

Press-mould or press To make shapes by pressing sheets of clay, patted, rolled or cut from blocks, into or onto moulds normally made of biscuited clay or plaster of Paris. Handles and spouts, as well as dishes and pots made from one or more moulds, are made in this way.

Pulling (handles) Plastic clay is stroked with water by hand to shape handles, either directly on the pot from a lump stuck on the side, or by pulling (shaping) a rudimentary handle which is completed later, once attached to the pot.

Raku Low-fired earthenware, glazed with lead or alkaline glazes; traditionally made in Japan for the tea ceremony. The pots are taken from the still-firing kiln and plunged into water, sometimes having been previously dropped into vegetation to reduce the metal oxides and so give different colour results.

Raw glazing See page 94. Glazing unfired pots, the biscuit firing is omitted and the glazes must contain enough clay in them to stay on the pots as they shrink during the single-firing.

Reduction Firing a kiln with a reducing atmosphere; the condition in a kiln if not enough air is supplied to burn completely the carbon particles and compounds in the flame, giving a smokey atmosphere. This process causes coppers to turn red, small amounts of iron to go green, and in higher firings, iron pyrites in the clay to give a characteristic speckled look.

Refractory Resistant to heat, capable of standing high temperatures in the range of 1300°C plus.

Sgraffito A decorating technique. A layer of slip is scratched through to reveal a different colour of clay or body beneath.

Slabbing A hand-building technique involving sheets of clay which can be rolled round other forms, or cut and jointed as in woodwork to make hard-edged forms.

Slip Liquid clay, often used with added metal oxides for colouring, or other materials to make it more, or less, vitreous. Pots can be dipped in slip or it can be poured, painted or trailed on to the surface.

Soak To hold the temperature in a kiln steady for some time.

Soft-paste Imitation porcelain. The body was a glass frit fired at around 1100°C. See *Porcelain*.

Stoneware Pottery which is opaque, hard and usually vitreous or non-porous, fired above 1200°C.

Tenmoku The Japanese name given to the glaze first produced in China. It usually contains at least 7% or 8% iron oxide to give a lustrous brown-black that breaks to orange-red where the glaze thins on edges and throwing rings.

Throwing Using the momentum of the potter's wheel to draw plastic clay into various circular forms.

Tooth Roughness or coarseness in a clay, a little can aid throwing, and counteract warping in handbuilding.

Turning Trimming pottery upside down on the wheel while it is leather-hard to remove excess clay and to form a foot-ring on the base of the pot.

Vitrify To fire or heat to a glassy state.

Volatilise To change into a vapour, oxides such as copper that do this at high temperatures are often deposited elsewhere in the kiln, on shelves or other pots.

A book may help you to take up pottery but it cannot replace a good teacher; so if you decide to try the craft of pottery it is best to seek instruction. A few practising potters actually run classes in their potteries throughout the year or at specific times; Local Education Authorities will be able to give you the addresses of adult education classes, and a few Schools of Art still give room to part-time day and evening students. If you wish to take up pottery as a full-time profession the D.E.S. has a list of the vocational and B.A. courses available.

In the United Kingdom, museums all over the country, ranging from the small county museums which often house surprising treasures, to the large Nationals like the Victoria and Albert Museum, have a comprehensive selection of work from all periods and places. Galleries and shops display and sell the work of contemporary potters, often holding exhibitions of individual potters' work. There are guilds and other organisations some of which publish magazines or newsletters. So there are many ways of extending your interest in pottery – working at your own techniques, studying pots old and new, reading and discussion. You will find there is always more to learn about the craft of the potter.

Booklist

General

BILLINGTON, D. M. *The technique of pottery* rev. edn. by J. Colbeck. Batsford, 1975.
CARDEW, M. *Pioneer pottery* Longman, 1969; n.e. paperback 1971.
CLARK, Lord *Practical pottery and ceramics* Studio Vista, paperback 1972.
COOPER, E. *Pottery* Macdonald, 1976.
DICKERSON, J. *Pottery making: a complete guide* Nelson, 1974.
FIELDHOUSE, M. *Pottery* Foyle, 1952.
GREEN, D. *Experimenting with pottery* Faber, 1971.
LEACH, B. *A potter's book* Faber, 1945; n.e. paperback 1976.
WINKLEY, D. *Pottery* Pelham Books, 1974.

Specialised

BECK, C. *Stoneware glazes* Isles House Publications, P.O. Box 61, Burnley, 1973.
COLBECK, J. *Pottery: the technique of throwing* Batsford, 1969.
DRAKE, K. *Simple pottery* Studio Vista, 1966.
(Covers handbuilding well.)
FRASER, H. *Glazes for the craft potter* Pitman, 1973.
GREBANIER, J. P. *Making Chinese stoneware glazes* Pitman, 1975.
LYNGGAARD, F. *Pottery: Raku technique* Van Nostrand Reinhold, hard and paperback 1973.
PARMELEE, C. W. *Ceramic glazes* Chicago: Industrial Publications, 1948. op (Highly technical.)
PLOWMAN, T. *Craft pottery* Shire Publications, 1976.
(Mainly about a thrower's workshop.)
RHODES, D. *Clay and glazes for the potter* Pitman, 2nd rev. edn. 1973.
(Good simple introduction to the chemistry and materials of pottery.)
RHODES, D. *Stoneware and porcelain* Pitman, 1960.
(Chemistry and techniques.)
RIEGGER, H. *Primitive pottery* Van Nostrand Reinhold, 1973.
(Handbuilding techniques.)
RIEGGER, H. *Raku: art and technique* Studio Vista, 1970. op.
SHAFTER, T. *Pottery decoration* Watson-Guptill: Pitman, 1976.
Pitmans skills series – individual books including handbuilding, porcelain, salt-glazing, etc.

Historical and contemporary pottery

BIRKS, T. *The art of the modern potter* Country Life, 1970. op.
CAIGER-SMITH, A. *Tin glaze pottery in Europe and the Islamic world: the tradition of 1000 years in Maiolica, Faience and Delftware* Faber, 1973. (There are many other titles in this wide-ranging series of Faber monographs on pottery and porcelain.)
CAMERON, E. and LEWIS, P. *Potters on pottery* Evans Bros, 1976.
CASSON, M. *Pottery in Britain today* Tiranti, 1967.

CHARLESTON, R. J. ed. *World ceramics* Hamlyn, 1968.
COOPER, E. *A history of pottery* Longman, 1972.
COOPER, R. G. *English slipware dishes, 1600-1850* Tiranti, 1968.
LEHMANN, H. *Pre-Columbian ceramics* Elek, 1962, op.
LEWENSTEIN, E. and COOPER, E. eds. *New ceramics* Studio Vista, 1974.
ROSE, M. *Artist potters in England* Faber, 1970.
WILLETTS, W. *The foundations of Chinese art* Thames and Hudson, 1965. op.
Publications of the Ashmolean Museum, Oxford.
Publications of the Victoria and Albert Museum, London.

Dictionaries

FOURNIER, R. *Illustrated dictionary of practical pottery* Van Nostrand Reinhold, 1973.
HAMER, F. *The potter's dictionary of materials and techniques* Pitman, 1975.

Philosophy

LEACH, B. *A potter in Japan* Faber, 1960. op.
LEACH, B. *A potter's challenge* Souvenir Press, 1976.
LEACH, B. *A potter's portfolio* Lund Humphries, 1951. op.
LEACH, B. *Drawings, verse and belief* Adams and Dart, 1973.
RAWSON, P. *Ceramics* (Appreciation of the arts) OUP, hard and paperback 1971.
YANAGI, S. *The unknown craftsman: Japanese insight into beauty* trans. by B. Leach. Kodansha International, US, 1973.
NB n.e: new edition; o.p: out of print

Magazines

Crafts bi-monthly published by C.A.C.
Ceramic Review bi-monthly published by C.P.A.
Pottery Quarterly Murray Fieldhouse, Northfields Studio, Northfields, Tring, Herts.

Suppliers of clay and equipment advertise in the above, if you are unable to get the material you want from your local craft shop. Many suppliers will send a free catalogue, which, as well as listing their equipment, gives a lot of useful additional information.

Residential short courses, published by the National Institute of Adult Education, is available from Research Publication Services, Victoria Hall, East Greenwich, London SE10 0RF.

Britain: holiday courses, published by the British Tourist Authority and available from BTA Sales Counter, 4 Bromells Road, London, SW4 0BJ, lists some pottery courses.

Floodlight, published by the Inner London Education Authority, is available from the GLC Bookshop, County Hall, London SE1 and through newsagents and bookshops. It lists pottery courses in London beginning each year in September.

Try your Public Library and your Local Education Authority, both may have details of pottery courses in your area.

Useful addresses

Crafts Advisory Committee (C.A.C.) 12 Waterloo Place, London SW1Y 4AU.
British Crafts Centre 43 Earlham St., London WC2H 9LD.
Craftsmen Potters' Association (C.P.A.) William Blake House, 7 Marshall St., London W1V 1FD; publishes *Potters; an illustrated directory of the work of its full members; and a guide to pottery training in Britain* 3rd edn. edited by E. Cooper, 1976.
Federation of British Craft Societies 6 Queen Square, London, WC1N 3AR.

Key to back cover photographs

1 Porcelain teapot by David Leach, brush painted decoration
2 Stoneware cooking pot with ash glaze drip by John Leach
3 Pinched porcelain pot by Mary Rogers
4 Pre-Columbian handbuilt pot with painted monster decoration, about 7th century AD
5 Blue and white porcelain dish Chinese Yuan dynasty, 14th century
6 Alan Caiger-Smith painting a bowl with cobalt pigment